Psalm 82

The Divine Council of the Gods, the Judgment of the Watchers & the Inheritance of the Nations

By Brian Godawa

Psalm 82: The Divine Council of the Gods, The Judgment of the Watchers and the Inheritance of the Nations
5th Expanded Edition

Warrior Poet Publishing
www.warriorpoetpublishing.com

ISBN: 978-1-942858-40-9 (paperback)
ISBN: 978-1-942858-41-6 (ebook)

Scripture quotations taken from The Holy Bible: English Standard Version. Wheaton: Standard Bible Society, 2001, except where noted as the NASB: New American Standard Bible: 1995 Update. (LaHabra, CA: The Lockman Foundation, 1995).

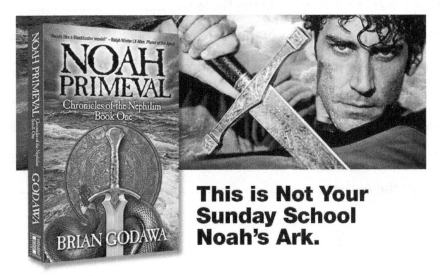

Table of Contents

Chapter 1:
The Divine Council of the Gods

One of the most intriguing storylines of the Bible is that of Christ's victory over the powers. When I discovered it, it changed my life. It inspired me to write a series of 14+ biblical novels—*Chronicles of the Nephilim*, *Chronicles of the Apocalypse* and *Chronicles of the Watchers*—that incarnate that story unlike anything done before.

A Definition

But what exactly is this messianic cosmic battle between Christ and the powers? And how does it affect us? It is sometimes called Christus Victor, and consists of the idea that mankind's Fall in the Garden resulted in a sinfulness of humanity that was so entrenched against God it led to universal idolatry as embodied in the tower of Babel story (Gen 11). As a result of man's incorrigible evil, God placed all of the nations and their lands under the authority of other spiritual powers, but kept one people and their land for his own: Israel. Those Gentile nations and their gods would be at war with the promised messianic seed of Israel. But in the fullness of time, Messiah would arrive, overcome those spiritual powers of the nations, and take back rule of the earth in the kingdom of God.

Gods or Men?

Psalm 82 is a doorway into the Christus Victor narrative because it summarizes the three-act structure of that messianic story of allotment, judgment and inheritance. Here is the full text of the Psalm in all its simple and concise glory:

Psalm 82:1–8
God has taken his place in the divine council;
>in the midst of the gods he holds judgment:
"How long will you judge unjustly
>and show partiality to the wicked? *Selah*
Give justice to the weak and the fatherless;
>maintain the right of the afflicted and the destitute.
Rescue the weak and the needy;
>deliver them from the hand of the wicked."
They have neither knowledge nor understanding,
>they walk about in darkness;
>all the foundations of the earth are shaken.
I said, "You are gods,
>sons of the Most High, all of you;
nevertheless, like men you shall die,
>and fall like any prince."
Arise, O God, judge the earth;
>for you shall inherit all the nations!

Much scholarly debate has occurred over the identity of these "gods" of the divine council. Are they human judges who merely represent divine justice, or are they actual divine beings?

I am convinced that they are Yahweh's heavenly host of divine beings surrounding his throne, referred to by the technical term "Sons of God" or "Sons of the Most High". Here's why…

Gods, Not Men

First off, the Psalm itself uses the Hebrew word *elohim,* which is accurately translated as "gods." As much as Christians have been conditioned to believe the Bible claims no other gods exist but Yahweh, this simply is not biblical. But don't panic. Hear me out.

The most common Hebrew word translated in English as "God" or "gods" in the Bible is *elohim*. But God has many names in the text and each of them is used to describe different aspects of his person. *El*, often refers to God's powerful preeminence; *El Elyon* (God Most High) indicates God as possessor of heaven and earth; *Adonai* means God as lord or master; and *Yahweh* is the covenantal name for the God of Israel as distinguished from any other deity.

Elohim in Hebrew is a plural word. It is used of both the singular being of the One God, as well as of a plurality of other beings who are not the singular One God. That is where some confusion comes into interpretation. Our modern Western English language does not translate the ancient Hebrew conceptual world very well at all. Here is a good example: In the biblical Hebrew, angels are sometimes called *elohim* (Psa 8:5; Heb 2:7), gods or idols of pagan nations are sometimes called *elohim* (Psa 138:1), supernatural beings of the divine council are sometimes called *elohim* (Psa 82:6), departed spirits of humans are sometimes called *elohim* (1Sam 28:13), and demons are sometimes called *elohim* (Deut 32:17).[1] So what gives? How can all these different entities be called by the same word—and a word that is also used of the One God?

Scholar Michael S. Heiser has pointed out that the Hebrew word *Elohim* was more of a reference to a plane of existence than to a substance of being. In this way, Yahweh was *Elohim*, but no other *elohim* was Yahweh. Yahweh is incomparably THE *Elohim* of *elohim* (Deut. 10:17).[2] We must stop imposing our categories of modern concepts onto the Bible, and try to interpret the text within the ancient Hebrew paradigm.

A common misunderstanding of Christians is that when the Bible refers to other gods it does not mean that the gods are real beings but merely

---

[1] Geoffrey W. Bromiley, "God, Names of," *The International Standard Bible Encyclopedia, Revised.* Wm. B. Eerdmans, 1988; 2002, p. 504-508.
[2] Michael S. Heiser, *The Myth That is True: Rediscovering the Cosmic Narrative of the Bible*, unpublished manuscript, 2011, p 25-29. Available online at www.michaelsheiser.com. I have read quite a few scholars on the divine council, but Michael Heiser has been the most helpful and represents the major influence on this essay.

beliefs in real beings that do not exist. For instance, when Deuteronomy 32:43 proclaims "rejoice with him, O heavens, bow down to him, all gods," this is a poetic way of saying "what you believe are gods are not gods at all because Yahweh is the only God that exists." What seems to support this interpretation is the fact that a few verses before this (v. 39), God says, "See now, that I, even I am he, and there is no god [*elohim*] beside me."

Does this not clearly indicate that God is the only God [*elohim*] that really exists out of all the non-existent "gods" [*elohim*] that others believe in?

Not in its biblical context it doesn't.

When the text is examined in its full context of the chapter and rest of the Bible we discover a very different notion about God and gods. The phrase "I am, and there is none beside me" was an ancient Biblical slogan of incomparability of sovereignty, not exclusivity of existence. It was a way of saying that a certain authority was the most powerful *compared to* all other authorities. It did not mean that there were no other authorities that existed.

We see this sloganeering in two distinct passages, one of the ruling power of Babylon claiming proudly in her heart, "I am, and there is no one beside me" (Isa. 47:8) and the other of the city of Nineveh boasting in her heart, "I am, and there is no one else" (Zeph. 2:15). The powers of Babylon and Nineveh are obviously not saying that there are no other powers or cities that exist other than them, because they had to conquer other cities and rule over them. "No other beside me" meant "no other equal in power or authority." God is seated on his throne of authority and power and there is no one standing beside him on that throne, having equal status. All others are "below" him. In the same way,

Yahweh uses that colloquial phrase, not to deny the existence of other gods, but to express his incomparable sovereignty over them.[3]

The Hebrew word for "gods," *elohim*, is plural but it is not polytheistic. Sometimes, it is a reference to created yet divine beings that we generically refer to as "angels." They are also biblically referred to as "holy ones" (Deut 33:2-3; Heb 2:2), "host of heaven" (1 King 22:19-23), or "Sons of God" (Job 1:6; 38:7). These Sons of God or host of heaven are called elohim, or "gods" in Psalm 82 and elsewhere in the Bible.

Psalm 89 clarifies this "assembly of gods" as being divine, not human, because it is in the heavens, not on earth.

> Psalm 89:5-7
> Let the heavens praise your wonders, O Yahweh,
> your faithfulness in the assembly of the holy ones!
> For who in the skies can be compared to Yahweh?
> Who among the gods is like Yahweh,
> a God greatly to be feared in the council of the holy
> ones,
> and awesome above all who are around him?

In this text, we see that there is an assembly of gods/holy ones who surround Yahweh in the heavens. These are clearly not humans on earth. And humans are not assembled in the skies. The text explicitly calls the assembly of Yahweh's holy ones "gods." But it uses the hypothetical question of incomparability with Yahweh, "who among the gods is like Yahweh?" The implied answer is none of them.

---

[3] Michael S. Heiser, "Monotheism, Polytheism, Monolatry, or Henotheism? Toward an Assessment of Divine Plurality in the Hebrew Bible" (2008). Faculty Publications and Presentations. Paper 277, p. 12-15, http://digitalcommons.liberty.edu/cgi/viewcontent.cgi?article=1276&context=lts_fac_pubs&sei-redir=1#search=%22heiser+Monotheism,+Polytheism,+Monolatry,+or+Henotheism%22 accessed March 23, 2011.

But they are still called gods (*elohim*), not "as gods," not "like gods," but gods. Here are several other passages that reiterate this idea of gods as real spiritual divine beings.

> Psalm 29:1
> Ascribe to the LORD, O gods, ascribe to the LORD glory and strength.

> Psalm 58:1-2
> Do you indeed decree what is right, you gods? Do you judge the children of man uprightly? No, in your hearts you devise wrongs; your hands deal out violence on earth.

> Deuteronomy 32:43
> "Rejoice with him, O heavens; bow down to him, all gods..."

Some may argue that these are verses that merely speak metaphorically of pagan gods bowing down to Yahweh in power because they do not actually exist. But as we have seen, the "gods" that these passages are talking about, are referring to the heavenly host, not necessarily pagan deities. These are real gods that have some actual relational interaction with Yahweh.

Notice that Psalm 58:1-2 is a restatement of the Psalm 82 notion of the gods who fail to judge the nations righteously. That is not a metaphor either, that is real relational interaction that Yahweh is claiming. He has given these gods some kind of authority over human beings. We will see exactly what kind of authority that is in the next chapter, but for now, suffice it to say these gods are described as real beings that Yahweh is interacting with.

So, there you have it. The Bible's definition of "gods," is not the same as our modern cultural religious definition of gods. The Bible itself says that there are gods, but they are not the same kind of deity as Yahweh.

They are created gods. Yahweh is uncreated and the eternal creator of all other beings. This is something that makes evangelical Christians skittish, but something one must accept if one accepts the evangelical principle of Sola Scriptura. If the Bible says it, it's true, regardless of where our preconceived biases may lean. Our fears are often expressions of our own lack of knowledge.

But there are some who argue that these "gods" are actually human judges who are called "gods" symbolically because they represent God in their identities as judges using God's Law. They argue that Moses was told that he would "be as God" to both Pharaoh and Aaron because he spoke on God's behalf (Ex 7:1; 4:16).

This cannot possibly be the case. First, there is a BIG difference between being called "gods" (*elohim*) and "being as God." The first is identity; the second is analogy.

Secondly, as Psalm 82 declares, these *elohim* (gods) are in God's divine council, which elsewhere is also described explicitly as a council of spiritual beings, not human beings (Job 1, 2; 1 King 22:19-23).

Thirdly, this assembly is "in the skies," or heaven, not on earth where human judges would be.

Fourthly, their punishment of death "like any earthly prince" is made in ironic contrast to being divine (Psalm 82:6-7). That punishment would be a meaningless tautology if the "gods" were actually human. The text does not say they would die *as* men, but that they would die *like* men. This is a statement of simile, not identity; it suggests a different ontological nature between gods and men.

The basic argument for the "gods" being human judges seeks to make the term (and its equivalent, "Sons of God") a symbolic analogy rather than an essential identity. They quote a verse like the following to justify this belief:

2 Chronicles 19:5-6
He appointed judges in the land in all the fortified cities
of Judah, city by city, and said to the judges, "Consider
what you do, for you judge not for man but for the
LORD. He is with you in giving judgment."

This view claims that because the judges are given authority by God to make legal judgments, and those judgments are "for the Lord," then judges could be considered gods in that they stand in the place of God, and he endorses their judgments. In this view, "gods" is a term of analogy, not identity.

But there are significant problems with this interpretation. The biggest one is that the text never calls those judges "gods." That is imported by the bias of the one seeking to justify the claim. It is a smuggled premise that begs the question. They are, in fact, not called gods anywhere in the text; God is "with them" in their judgments, but that is not the same as being called gods. In contrast, the beings of the divine council are explicitly called gods.

Even in today's legal system, we do the same thing as described in 2 Chronicles. When we stand in a court of law presided over by a judge and pledge to tell the truth before God, we are claiming that God resides behind the judge and court in their pursuit of justice. But we are not pledging to the judge as a "god," or even as God's representative; we are pledging to the actual God who stands transcendently behind the court. Yes, the judge has God's authority to make his judgments (Rom 13:1-2), but we do not call him a god in his representation. Our pledge is to the God who is actually and truly behind the judge, not to the judge as if he were in place of God.

The significance of the term "gods" being used of the beings in the divine council is a reference to their divine identity, not their representational authority.

Another problem with this human interpretation of "gods" is projection, or what I like to call "hermeneutical imperialism." Hermeneutics is the science and art of interpreting a text; that is, interpreters do not interpret the text within the context of the original writers and readers, but rather within their own modern context, which results in projecting their own cultural bias onto the text instead of discovering the cultural bias *within* the text.

If we want to understand how the ancient Jews understood the terms they used, we should look at how they themselves interpreted the texts. If one uses only Scripture to interpret Scripture without its cultural context, then one is not actually using Scripture to interpret Scripture, but conforming Scripture to one's own cultural bias and preconceived ideas.

When we look at the ancient Jewish understanding of Psalm 82, we see the gods as divine beings, not human.

In the Dead Sea Scrolls, an ancient Jewish document labeled 11QMelchizedek reveals that they understood the gods of Psalm 82 to be satanic spirits to whom God allotted the nations.

> 11QMelchizedek 2.10-16
> As for that which he said, How long will you judge unjustly and show partiality to the wicked? Selah (Psalms 82:2), its interpretation concerns Satan and the spirits of his lot who rebelled by turning away from the precepts of God to…And Melchizedek will avenge the vengeance of the judgements of God…and he will drag them from the hand of Satan and from the hand of all the spirits of his lot. And all the 'gods of Justice' will come to his aid to attend to the destruction of Satan.[4]

---

[4] Geza Vermes, *The Dead Sea Scrolls in English, Revised and extended 4th ed.* (Sheffield: Sheffield Academic Press, 1995), 361.

Now, there were certainly a variety of theological viewpoints in Judaism, but this text does illustrate the dominant divine interpretation of that ancient context.

Here is another text from a well-known noncanonical Jewish text that interprets the Sons of God in Deuteronomy 32:8-10 as also being angels or territorial spirits spoken of in Psalm 82.

> Jubilees 15:31-32
>
> [There are] many nations and many people, and they all belong to him, but over all of them he caused spirits to rule so that they might lead them astray from following him. But over Israel he did not cause any angel or spirit to rule because he alone is their ruler and he will protect them.

This passage from Jubilees is actually an interpretation of Deuteronomy 32:8-10 that I will explore in the next chapter. But the point here is that the Sons of God in Deuteronomy were considered to be the same divine spirits who ruled over and judged the nations in Psalm 82. They were decidedly *not* human judges.

But there is another ancient interpreter of Psalm 82 that settles the argument over the divine identity of the gods/Sons of God. And that exegetical expert is none other than *the* Son of God.

What Would Jesus Exegete?

My personal view is that if the Bible says it, then we should say it. I am fine with using the term "divine beings" if it makes you feel more comfortable, but the bottom line is that the Sons of God who surround Yahweh's heavenly throne as his host are divine. The Bible calls them gods.

Jesus, God in the flesh, used this very Psalm to justify his claims to deity in John 10:31-39. So if Jesus's own exegesis of Psalm 82 results in ascribing divinity to the gods, then we need to agree with the author and finisher of our faith.

First, let's look at the context. Jesus says to the Jews listening to him, "I and the Father are one" (John 10:30). He did not mean "one in purpose," but rather "one in essence or identity." We know this because the Jews respond by picking up stones to stone Jesus (v. 31). They understood him as engaging in blasphemy and accused him, "because you, being a man, make yourself God" (v. 33). So Jesus answers by appealing to Psalm 82.

> John 10:34–36
>
> Jesus answered them, "Is it not written in your Law, 'I said, you are gods'? If he called them gods to whom the word of God came—and Scripture cannot be broken—do you say of him whom the Father consecrated and sent into the world, 'You are blaspheming,' because I said, 'I am the Son of God'?

Some say that those "gods" in Psalm 82 are simply human judges who represent God. But Jesus is clearly claiming actual deity with his term Son of God, not mere representation. He did not claim to be a representative human judge like other Israelite judges. That would have been a denial of his deity, degrading him to the level of human judges.

That would contradict the very point he was making at the start by saying "I and the Father are one" in essence or identity. He would be claiming that he is no different from human judges who represent God and that "Son of God" is a term of representation, not identity or essence. Shame on trinitarians for even considering such a contradiction.

If Jesus had intended his reference to the sons of God to represent nothing more than mere human judges, then he would have been ascribing to his own sonship no more authority or divinity than that held by human judges. He would have been denying deity, not arguing for it. His claim to be the Son of God would be stripped of its divine essence. That would be worse than nonsense; it would be blasphemous nonsense.

I think it's clear that Jesus was claiming to be divine in this passage. He was defining Sons of God as actual divine beings, not representative human judges. And his point in quoting Psalm 82 was to prove to them that his own claim to divinity was not blasphemous because they already accepted some beings other than Yahweh as having divinity. Jesus was not merely one of those divine Sons of God, he was THE uniquely begotten Son of God, God in the flesh.

Job

This heavenly assembly of gods is not an anomaly. It shows up in many places throughout the Bible that indicate a clear context of spiritual beings who engage in council with Yahweh and carry out his judgments. A heavenly legal courtroom.

Job 1:6 and 2:1 describe an apparently regular occurrence of "Sons of God" (*bene ha elohim* in Hebrew) presenting themselves before Yahweh, along with the satan as legal adversary in that heavenly court.

> Job 1:6-7, 12
> Now there was a day when the sons of God came to present themselves before the LORD, and Satan also came among them. The LORD said to Satan, "From where have you come?" Satan answered the LORD and said, "From going to and fro on the earth, and from walking up and down on it"… And the LORD said to the satan, "Behold, all that [Job] has is in your hand. Only against him do not stretch out your hand." So the satan went out from the presence of the LORD.

The satan operates as a spiritual prosecutor in God's heavenly court seeking indictment of righteous Job by accusing him of self-interest in serving God. God then allows him to carry out a task in order to test Job. But it is important to note that this is not an earthly court with humans, but a heavenly court in God's presence.

These sons of God are not human judges, but God's heavenly host. And this is confirmed later in Job, lest there be any doubt. God chastises Job from the whirlwind and he asks him, "Where were you when I laid the foundation of the earth?... when the morning stars sang together and all the sons of God shouted for joy?" (Job 38:4–7).

Yahweh himself states that the Sons of God were present at the creation of the heavens and earth, shouting for joy (Job 38:7) long *before* human judges were created.

These Sons of God also show up in Psalm 82 as "Sons of the Most High."

> Psalm 82:6
> I said, "You are gods,
>   sons of the Most High, all of you;

"Sons of the Most High" is a synonym for "Sons of God." "Most High" in Hebrew is *El Elyon*, another name of Yahweh. God has many names: Elohim, Yahweh, El Elyon, El Shaddai and so forth. So the gods around him have several names: gods, heavenly host, holy ones, Sons of God and Sons of the Most High. Sons of the Most High in Psalm 82 is interchangeable with Sons of God.

Sons of God/Most High is not a mere metaphor, as in "we are all children of God," but rather it is a technical term used only of this special class of being. Though some argue that Israel is called the son of God, this is simply not true. The passage they quote says, "When Israel was a child, I loved him, and out of Egypt I called my son" (Hos 11:1). Yes, in this case "son" is used of Israel as a metaphor, but it is not the term "son of God" or "sons of God". That is a very important distinction, because when Jesus claimed to be the Son of God, the Jews were offended by this as a claim of deity (John 10:36). This would not be the case if "Son(s) of God" were a mere metaphor like the word "son" that Hosea uses. There are many presidents in America, but there is only one President of the United States. The technical term "sons of God/Most High" is highly specific, not a generic metaphor like "son".

These are the same Sons of God that left their heavenly habitation and came to earth and mated with the human daughters of men.

> Genesis 6:1–2
> ¹ When man began to multiply on the face of the land
> and daughters were born to them, ² the sons of God saw
> that the daughters of man were attractive. And they
> took as their wives any they chose.

This passage is also a highly debated one. Many interpreters also argue that these Sons of God in Genesis 6 are humans from the lineage of Seth or despotic god-kings.

Space does not permit a full defense here of the supernatural nature of the Sons of God in Genesis 6 (see my book *When Giants Were Upon the Earth* for a fully developed argument). But I will make the point that both New Testament inspired authors Peter and Jude considered those Sons of God in Genesis 6 to be divine angels.

> Jude 6–7 (NASB95)
> And **angels** who did not keep their own domain, but
> abandoned their proper abode, He has kept in eternal
> bonds under darkness for the judgment of the great day,
> just as Sodom and Gomorrah and the cities around
> them, since they in the same way as these indulged in
> gross immorality and went after strange flesh…

> 2 Peter 2:4–5
> For if God did not spare **angels** when they sinned, but
> cast them into hell and committed them to chains of

gloomy darkness to be kept until the judgment; if he
did not spare the ancient world, but preserved Noah, a
herald of righteousness, with seven others, when he
brought a flood upon the world of the ungodly…

Peter places this angelic sin at the time of the Flood. The only possible biblical reference to this sin is the wicked behavior of the Sons of God in Genesis 6 marrying women by force.

> Genesis 6:1–10
> When man began to multiply on the face of the land
> and daughters were born to them, the sons of God saw
> that the daughters of man were attractive. And they
> took as their wives any they chose… The LORD saw
> that the wickedness of man was great in the earth, and
> that every intention of the thoughts of his heart was
> only evil continually.

Some try to deny the negative connotations of the behavior of the sons of God in this passage. I deal with that more extensively in When Giants Were Upon the Earth. But for now, let me make the point that the dominant view in the ancient Jewish mindset (including the New Testament) was that the Sons of God were angels who sinfully defied the heavenly/earthly boundaries.

Both Peter and Jude speak of the sin of the angels in the same context as Sodom and Gomorrah. Jude calls them angels who "indulged in gross immorality and went after strange flesh." "Strange flesh" cannot mean homosexuality in this passage, because the Greek words are *heteros sarx* (different flesh). Homosexuality would be same flesh (*homo sarx*). The "strange flesh" here must be a difference of flesh between angels and humans. The sin of Sodom, linked to the sin of the angels in Noah's time, was not men desiring sex with men so much as it was humans desiring sex with angels (Genesis 6 all over again).

The Sodom story was not merely known in Second Temple Judaism as an example of homosexuality, but was linked with Genesis 6 as an example of humans trying to have sinful sex with angels who had a heavenly flesh different from human flesh.

> Testament of Naphtali 3:4-5
> …so that you do not become like Sodom, which departed from the order of nature. Likewise the Watchers departed from nature's order; the Lord pronounced a curse on them at the Flood.[5]

> Jubilees 10:1, 5
> The polluted demons began to lead astray the children of Noah's sons and to lead them to folly and to destroy them… [Noah prayed,] [6]"And Thou knowest how Thy Watchers, the fathers of these spirits, acted in my day: and as for these spirits which are living, imprison them and hold them fast in the place of condemnation."

Though The Testament of Naphtali and the book of Jubilees are not Scripture, they were highly regarded Jewish writings that expressed the dominant ancient Jewish view, which was echoed in the first century by the Jewish historian Josephus, who wrote of Genesis 6 that "many angels of God accompanied with women, and begat sons that proved unjust, and despisers of all that was good."[7]

If New Testament apostolic authority exegetes the sin of Genesis to be that of divine angelic beings, in accord with the ancient Jewish worldview, then I think we are biblically safe to agree with them.

---

[5] Charlesworth, James H. *The Old Testament Pseudepigrapha: Volume 1*. New York; London: Yale University Press, 1983, 812.
[6] James H. Charlesworth, *The Old Testament Pseudepigrapha and the New Testament: Expansions of the "Old Testament" and Legends, Wisdom, and Philosophical Literature, Prayers, Psalms and Odes, Fragments of Lost Judeo-Hellenistic Works*, vol. 2 (New Haven; London: Yale University Press, 1985), 75.
[7] Flavius Josephus, *Antiquities of the Jews* 1:73.

1 Kings 22

My personal favorite Sons of God passage is the story of wicked king Ahab asking for the prophet Micaiah's advice on attacking Ramoth-Gilead. Micaiah describes a scenario so obviously supernatural and spiritual that little explanation is required. Though the beings in the council here are not described as "gods" like elsewhere, they are described as the "host of heaven," which we have already shown the Bible defines as divine beings or gods (Jer 19:13; Deut 4:19; 17:3; 29:26; 2 Chron 33:3-5; Acts 7:42-43).

> 1 Kings 22:19–23
> And Micaiah said, "Therefore hear the word of the LORD: I saw the LORD sitting on his throne, and all the host of heaven standing beside him on his right hand and on his left; and the LORD said, 'Who will entice Ahab, that he may go up and fall at Ramoth-Gilead?' And one said one thing, and another said another. Then a spirit came forward and stood before the LORD, saying, 'I will entice him.' And the LORD said to him, 'By what means?' And he said, 'I will go out, and will be a lying spirit in the mouth of all his prophets.' And he said, 'You are to entice him, and you shall succeed; go out and do so.' Now therefore behold, the LORD has put a lying spirit in the mouth of all these your prophets; the LORD has declared disaster for you."

The fascinating thing about this vision is that we get a glimpse into the actual process of counseling that God takes from his heavenly host. We see them suggest different things, and then God chooses one and empowers the spirit to accomplish his task.

It's all rather scandalous to a modern Christian mind that prefers a nice, simple and uncomplicated spiritual world where God sits on his throne and declares the end from the beginning without anyone's input. But biblical facts are the facts. God uses a bureaucracy of intermediary divine agents, called gods, Sons of God, heavenly host, or holy ones, with whom he interacts and engages counsel.

Or as the Psalm we've been looking at from the very start puts it:

Psalm 82:1
God has taken his place in the divine council;
in the midst of the gods he holds judgment:

There are plenty of other passages that describe the divine council of heavenly beings around Yahweh who counsel with him and carry out his decisions with duly delegated legal responsibility (Deut 32:43 LXX; Zech 2:13-3:7; Jer 23:18-22).

And there are other passages where the divine council is not mentioned, but scholars explain that the plural grammar of the speech and activity imply the heavenly court motif of God addressing the council (Gen 1:26; 11:3, 4, 7; Isa 6:8; 40:1; 41:21-23). It is so prevalent throughout the Bible that one can only deny it to one's theological detriment.

You can read more about this theological paradigm of the Sons of God in my book *When Giants Were Upon the Earth*. And you can read a story of how this divine council plays out in history in my novel series *Chronicles of the Nephilim*, *Chronicles of the Apocalypse* and *Chronicles of the Watchers*

In the next chapter, I will explain the allotment of the nations at Babel and how it begins this storyline of the rise and fall of the Watchers and their inheritance of the nations.

Chapter 2:
The Allotment of the Nations

In Chapter 1, I defined the biblical motif of Christus Victor as Christ's victory over the spiritual powers who ruled sinful mankind. I defined the divine council biblically as an assembly of gods, called "Sons of God," "holy ones," and "heavenly host" who surround Yahweh, engage in legal counsel with him and carry out his decisions.

But the next question is, how did man come under the rule and authority of these gods, these divine beings from Yahweh's heavenly host?

I am using Psalm 82 as a portal into this fascinating storyline of the Bible. So let's take a look again at what it says.

> Psalm 82:1–8
> God has taken his place in the divine council;
>   in the midst of the gods he holds judgment:
> "How long will you judge unjustly
>   and show partiality to the wicked? *Selah*
> Give justice to the weak and the fatherless;
>   maintain the right of the afflicted and the destitute.
> Rescue the weak and the needy;
>   deliver them from the hand of the wicked."

So we see that for some reason, God has given some of these members from his divine council authority to rule over mankind on earth as their judges. Where did this come from? Why would God do such a thing? Isn't God alone the judge of all the earth? And why is he blaming failure to rule on divine beings? Does that make them fallen angels?

To answer those questions, we need to go back to the beginning. Not Genesis 1, but rather the beginning of the allotment of the nations to the gods: back to the Tower of Babel. But instead of going straight to Genesis 11, which tells the story of Babel, we need to read what Moses reveals about Babel in Deuteronomy 32.

The Deuteronomy 32 Worldview

Deuteronomy 32 is famously known as the Song of Moses. In it, Moses sings a song of the story of Israel and how she had come to be God's chosen nation. He begins by glorifying God and then telling them to "remember the days of old" (v. 7).

> Deuteronomy 32:8–9
> When the Most High gave to the nations their
>   inheritance,
>   when he divided mankind,
> he fixed the borders of the peoples
>   according to the number of the sons of God.
> But the LORD's portion is his people,
>   Jacob his allotted heritage.

The context of this passage is the Tower of Babel incident in Genesis 11. It is the only "division of mankind" in the text of Genesis. Rebellious humanity sought divinity in unified rebellion, so God separated them by confusing their tongues, which divided them into the seventy nations described in Genesis 10. The incident at Babel led to the creation of nations and their ownership of those territorial lands as the "inheritance" of those peoples. Nations are essentially God's creation to protect mankind from destroying itself through idolatrous one-world global unity in wickedness.

The apostle Paul referred to this allotment of national boundaries in Acts 17:26 when he said that God "made from one man every nation of mankind to live on all the face of the earth, having determined allotted periods and the boundaries of their dwelling places." That "one man" from whom every nation was made is not Adam, but Noah, because the allotment of nations occurred at Babel, not the Garden.

But that's not all. Deuteronomy 32 says that the borders of those nations were fixed "according to the number of the Sons of God." That is, the Sons of God are in authority over these nations, both geographically and spiritually. This allotment is in contrast with Yahweh's allotment of Jacob. The seventy nations were allotted to the Sons of God, in the same way that Yahweh allotted to himself the nation of Israel, described as (the people of) "Jacob."

The Septuagint, or the Greek translation of the Old Testament from which Jesus and the apostles quoted, translates "Sons of God" in Deuteronomy 32:8 as "angels of God," thus again affirming that the ancient Jewish world understood those beings as divine, not human.

And allotment is used synonymously in the passage with inheritance and heritage. In fact, the inheritance or allotment of land is one of the major themes of the Old Testament. God promises the Land of Canaan as an inheritance to the twelve tribes of Israel.

> Joshua 11:23
> So Joshua took the whole land, according to all that the
> LORD had spoken to Moses. And Joshua gave it for an
> inheritance to Israel according to their tribal allotments.

Remember this important theological truth; it will come into play later: *allotment and inheritance are about land and ownership under the old covenant.*

Since Genesis 10 describes seventy nations, the number of the Sons of God here must be seventy to match those nations. Or maybe seventy groups of Sons of God. But who are these seventy chosen divine beings? They can't be the myriad of "ten thousands" of heavenly host usually described as being around Yahweh's throne (Deut 33:2-3; Dan

7:10). They are only seventy. Yet Psalm 82 clearly states that they are part of that divine council. Then, who are they?

Are the Sons of God in Psalm 82 Evil?

Psalm 82:3-4 describes these gods as being given responsibility to administer justice over the peoples. The commands that God gives them about not showing partiality, giving justice and rescuing the weak, are all expressions found in the Law and the Prophets (Deut 1:16-17; Jer 22:3; Prov 24:11). The gods over the nations were supposed to rule according to God's justice.

Another Psalm reflects the same injustice of the ruling gods and their guilt before God's Word.

> Psalm 58:1–2
> Do you indeed decree what is right, you gods? Do you
> judge the children of man uprightly? No, in your hearts
> you devise wrongs; your hands deal out violence on
> earth.

Shallow readings of both Psalm 82 and 58 give one the impression that these "gods" are good spiritual powers that are entrusted with authority, since God would not impose bad rulers, would he? And then it appears that they fail to rule justly and end in darkness, which leads to their punishment in 82:7 of "dying like men," or "falling" like any other earthly ruler. So they sound like good divine beings gone bad.

But I think this is not an accurate understanding. I will argue that the Sons of God who inherited the nations at Babel (Deut 32:8-9) and ruled those nations in antiquity (Psa 82:2-3) were already fallen and evil when they received their allotment. Here's why…

First, the dominant paradigm of the Old Testament is the single nation of Israel as set apart by Yahweh to be a light to the darkened world of the Gentile nations, considered as a whole to be against God (Isa 49:6;

22

Psa 2:1-2). All the nations worshipped gods that were not Yahweh. And even by the time of the New Testament, the Jews considered the word Gentile to be synonymous with sinner (Matt 5:47; 10:5; 18:17; Act 4:25-26). Paul writes in Galatians 2:15, "We ourselves are Jews by birth and not Gentile sinners." So the biblical understanding of "the nations" in Genesis 11, Deuteronomy 32 and Psalm 82 are Gentile nations who are idolaters. They do not worship Yahweh.

Second, let us not forget that all the nations created at Babel consisted of people in rebellion against Yahweh at the very start. The confusion of tongues and division of mankind was a judgment for sinful man who had sought deity with their pagan temples to the gods. So the context of Deuteronomy 32:8-10 is division as judgment, not as neutral separation.

Third, earlier in Deuteronomy, Moses clarifies God's command not to worship the heavenly host, defined interchangeably as both gods and as astronomical bodies (sun, moon and stars). *But he states that he allotted those gods to all the other peoples.*

> Deuteronomy 4:19–20
> And beware lest you raise your eyes to heaven, and when you see the sun and the moon and the stars, all the host of heaven, you be drawn away and bow down to them and serve them, things that Yahweh your <u>God has allotted to all the peoples under the whole heaven</u>. But <u>Yahweh has taken</u> you and brought you out of the iron furnace, out of Egypt, <u>to be a people of his own inheritance</u>.

This allotment of the gods/host of heaven to the peoples is reminiscent of the description of God "giving up" pagans to their idolatrous worship of creation in Romans 1.

> Romans 1:21–28
> For although they knew God, they did not honor him as God or give thanks to him, but they became futile in

their thinking, and their foolish hearts were darkened. Claiming to be wise, they became fools, and exchanged the glory of the immortal God for images resembling mortal man and birds and animals and creeping things. Therefore **God gave them up** in the lusts of their hearts to impurity, to the dishonoring of their bodies among themselves…For this reason **God gave them up** to dishonorable passions… And since they did not see fit to acknowledge God, **God gave them up** to a debased mind to do what ought not to be done.

The contrast of God setting apart Israel "to be a people for his own inheritance" in Deuteronomy 4:20 after the allotment of the heavenly host in verse 19 is a reiteration of the allotment contrast in Deuteronomy 32. These verses refer to the same allotted inheritance.

In Deuteronomy 4 it's clear that Yahweh did not give the nations to be ruled by righteous heavenly host who then fell through accepting undeserved worship. Rather, Yahweh gave the host of heaven to all the peoples to worship as their gods *because they were already idolaters*. He was "giving them up" to their idolatry and giving the false gods their own people to rule over.

On first glance the phrase "to all the peoples under the whole heaven," would appear to mean that God allotted the heavenly host to everyone, including Israelites. But the context contradicts that inclusion when Moses says, "But Yahweh has taken you (Israel) to be a people of his own inheritance." "All the peoples under the whole heaven" is contrasted with Israel, not included with her.

Another passage in Deuteronomy reinforces this notion of sinful nations allotted to fallen gods. In Deuteronomy 29:26 Moses tells the Israelites that when they entered the land of Canaan, they "went and served other gods and worshiped them, gods whom they had not known and whom he had not allotted to them." This passage affirms that God allotted these fallen gods of the heavenly host to the Gentile nations of Canaan.

So, why does Psalm 82 read as if these Sons of God were righteous beings to start? Well, I don't think it does. Look closer at the passage:

> Psalm 82:1–4
> God has taken his place in the divine council;
>> in the midst of the gods he holds judgment:
> "How long will you judge unjustly
>> and show partiality to the wicked? *Selah*
> Give justice to the weak and the fatherless;
>> maintain the right of the afflicted and the destitute.
> Rescue the weak and the needy;
>> deliver them from the hand of the wicked."

Verse one depicts Yahweh convening his council to judge the gods. Then he tells them, "How long will you judge unjustly and show partiality to the wicked?" So these gods *are already ruling unjustly* when God convenes the council. Then Yahweh commands those unjust gods to "give justice," "maintain rights," and "rescue the weak." So, the question is, why would God command wicked gods to rule justly?

I think it is the same principle involved with the giving of the Mosaic Law to humans. God did not give the Law to a righteous people, hoping they would keep it and then they failed to achieve that righteous obedience. Rather, God gave the law to an *already sinful* people to show them their sin and justify their condemnation (Rom 5:12-14). In the same way, God "gives up" fallen humanity to their fallen gods who rule over them in their fallen state. And then Yahweh justifies their judgment by commanding them to do justice—which they fail to live up to. Criminals are told to keep the law just as much as non-criminals are.

Though I am not dogmatic about the Sons of God being already fallen when they were allotted the nations, I would argue that if they were originally righteous, they must have fallen very quickly, maybe within a few years of Babel. Evidence of the earliest post-Flood civilization of which we know, ancient Sumer, already contains a developed sophisticated religion of idolatrous polytheism.

The earliest post-Flood cultures to which the Bible refers are all idolatrous and polytheistic to the core when we meet them: the Canaanites, the Egyptians, and the Amorites, from which God called Abraham (Gen 12). *We simply have no historical or biblical evidence of a period of righteous spiritual rulers or righteous worship of Yahweh after Babel.* If there was, it didn't last long enough to merit historical significance or inclusion in the Scriptures.

It makes more sense that Babel proved mankind's incorrigible depravity. Even after the Flood, they would not worship Yahweh. So Yahweh gave them over to the false gods they already worshipped. Since morality is inherently part of the creation and is not relative or subjective, even fallen angels who are awarded territory are still accountable for their behavior. The Sons of God could not claim they were just following orders or performing God's will at their spiritual Nuremburg Trial to come (Rom 9:19-23).

The Sons of God Are Also Called Watchers

One last aspect of the divine council is necessary to understand the big picture in Scripture: the Sons of God who have been allotted the Gentile nations are also called "Watchers," for the very simple reason that they were given the responsibility of watching over the nations to which they were allotted.

In Daniel 10:4-7 the prophet receives a vision at the Tigris River that includes a "man" described in terms reserved in Scripture for divine beings (see Ezekiel 1). Some scholars even argue he could be a pre-incarnate Jesus Christ.

That divine holy one then describes a scenario of heavenly "princes" at war.

Daniel 10:13; 20-21

"The <u>prince of the kingdom of Persia</u> withstood me twenty-one days, but Michael, one of the <u>chief princes,</u> came to help me, for I was left there with the kings of Persia..."

Then he said, "Do you know why I have come to you? But now I will return to fight against the <u>prince of Persia</u>; and when I go out, behold, the <u>prince of Greece</u> will come. [21] But I will tell you what is inscribed in the book of truth: there is none who contends by my side against these except <u>Michael, your prince.</u>

In this passage, we see that the notion of national principalities and powers ruling over earthly kingdoms continued even past the exile into Daniel's period. The previous prophecies of Daniel 2 and 7-8 had predicted Persia and Greece to be at war, as one kingdom was replaced by the other. But these princes in Daniel 10 are not the earthly rulers, but rather their heavenly counterparts. There is a spiritual prince of Persia, a spiritual prince of Greece, and Michael the archangel is considered the spiritual prince of Israel.

The biblical picture is that the heavenly and earthly rulers were tied together in unity, so that when there was a war on earth, there was a corresponding war in heaven. So much so, that the fates of both heaven and earth were linked. Here are a couple examples from Scripture that reinforce this theme:

In the time of the Judges when Israel fought the pagan kings of Canaan, the battle with Sisera at the river of Megiddo was described within the same paragraph from the perspectives of both heaven and earth.

Judges 5:19–20

"<u>The kings came, they fought</u>; then fought the kings of Canaan, at Taanach, by the waters of Megiddo; they

got no spoils of silver. <u>From heaven the stars fought,</u>
from their courses they fought against Sisera."

Identical language is used to link the fighting of the kings on earth with the fighting of heavenly stars. Again, remember, the heavenly host were often considered interchangeable with the heavenly rulers over the earth. When the kings on earth were at war, so were their allotted gods at war.

Another strong example of this equivalence between heavenly and earthly rulers is found in their predicted judgment in Isaiah, who describes a synchronized judgment of earthly kings and their heavenly rulers:

> Isaiah 24:21–23
> On that day the LORD will punish
> > <u>the host of heaven, in heaven,</u>
> > and <u>the kings of the earth, on the earth</u>.

Jeremiah also affirms the connection between earthly authorities and their heavenly principalities, when he prophesies Yahweh's judgment upon Egypt and her gods, including the high god, Amon, who was the patron deity of Thebes.

> Jeremiah 46:25
> Yahweh of hosts, the God of Israel, said: "Behold, I am
> bringing punishment upon <u>Amon of Thebes, and</u>
> <u>Pharaoh and Egypt and her gods and her kings.</u>

When Yahweh punishes heavenly rulers, he also punishes earthly rulers along with them, and vice versa.

But where do I get the idea that these heavenly rulers are called Watchers? Well, jumping back to Daniel 4, he has another vision where he tells us Watchers are holy ones that come down from heaven.

Daniel 4:13, 17

"I saw in the visions of my head as I lay in bed, and behold, a watcher, a holy one, came down from heaven…

The sentence is by the decree of the watchers, the decision by the word of the holy ones, to the end that the living may know that the Most High rules the kingdom of men and gives it to whom he will and sets over it the lowliest of men.'

The Watchers are called "holy ones" (Deut 33:2-3; Jude 14), which we saw in Chapter 1 is another name for the heavenly host (1King 22:19) of the divine council (Psa 82:1), who are also called the Sons of God (Job 5:1; 15:15). We also see another reference to God allotting earthly territories to whomever he wills. So all these terms refer to the same divine beings. Though we do not see the term Watchers used specifically in Daniel 10, we see those ruling principalities of the nations that are also synonymous with the ruling gods/Sons of God/heavenly host of Psalm 82 and Deuteronomy 32.

The Watchers are the fallen Sons of God given the allotment of the nations, both land and people, as their inheritance.

Host of Heaven

One aspect of the Watchers in the Bible and other ancient Near Eastern sacred literature is their identification with the stars and planets in the heavens. The original context of heavenly host in the Bible is one of war. The Hebrew term for "host" (*saba*) was used as a reference to warriors. The term "Lord of Hosts" was then a designation of Yahweh as warrior king.

Isaiah 13:4–5

The sound of a tumult is on the mountains
    as of <u>a great multitude!</u>
The sound of an uproar of kingdoms,
    of nations gathering together!
The Lord <u>of hosts</u> is mustering
    a <u>host for battle</u>.
They come from a distant land,
    from the end of the heavens,
the Lord and <u>the weapons of his indignation,</u>
    to destroy the whole land.

In this passage, Isaiah likens the earthly armies of Babylon as Yahweh's own weapons used upon another nation. God is using Babylon providentially as his own host of warriors.

But there is a heavenly host of warriors as well. In Joshua 5, we are introduced to the leader of that heavenly host. Joshua was preparing to besiege Jericho, when an armed man appeared before him. But this warrior was more than a man. He proclaimed, "I am the commander of the host of the LORD" (5:14). And then, that commander, who was most likely the Angel of Yahweh (Jesus), said the exact same words that Yahweh proclaimed to Moses from the burning bush, "Take off your sandals from your feet, for the place where you are standing is holy" (5:15). Yahweh is a warrior king of a heavenly host of armies.

In 2 Kings 6, the prophet Elisha and his young assistant see the army of Syria surrounding Samaria. The servant worries that they are outnumbered. But Elisha tells him that there are more who are with Israel than with Syria. He then asks Yahweh to show the young man the spiritual realm. "So the Lord opened the eyes of the young man, and he saw, and behold, the mountain was full of horses and chariots of fire all around Elisha" (6:17).

Seeing this military context of the "host" sheds light on Yahweh's reference to the Israelites leaving Egypt as a host. "And on that very day the LORD brought the people of Israel out of the land of Egypt by their hosts" (Exodus 12:51). In the story of the Exodus up until the Yam Suph crossing, Yahweh describes his people as the "host of Israel" in contrast with "Pharaoh and all his host of Egypt" (Exodus 14:17, 19-20). Anyone familiar with the story knows that the Israelites were not an army and they didn't fight against Pharaoh. They were the entire population of the Hebrews and other slaves, men, women and children. So why describe them in military terms as a "host"? Why would Yahweh use a military term for his civilian population? Because the entire Exodus is being framed by Yahweh as a war of gods and men. Israel vs. Egypt, Yahweh vs. Pharaoh and Yahweh vs. the gods of Egypt (see my book *The Spiritual World of Moses and Egypt* for further information) The glory of it all is that in this mighty spiritual war, the Israelites did not fight at all because Yahweh fought for them! As the Song of Moses declares,

Exodus 15:2–11

Yahweh is my strength and my song,
  and he has become my salvation…
Yahweh is a man of war;
  Yahweh is his name.
"Pharaoh's chariots and his host he cast into the sea,
  and his chosen officers were sunk in the Red Sea.
The floods covered them;
  they went down into the depths like a stone.
Your right hand, O Yahweh, glorious in power,
  your right hand, O Yahweh, shatters the enemy…
"Who is like you, O Yahweh, among the gods?

Who is like you, majestic in holiness,
  awesome in glorious deeds, doing wonders?

But war is not the only responsibility of Yahweh's heavenly host. They are also the millions who surround Yahweh's throne in heaven to glorify him and partake of his divine council as mentioned earlier in 1 Kings 22 and Job 1 and 2. Yahweh's heavenly host surround him, worship him (Nehemiah 9:6), but also counsel with him and then perform Yahweh's commands of tasks.

The question arises, how many are there of these heavenly host? Throughout the Bible, symbolic phrases are used to describe the numbers as innumerable, or uncountable. "Ten thousands" (plural) of these holy ones are depicted at Sinai (Deuteronomy 33:2). The New Testament author Jude quotes from 1 Enoch that says that the Lord will come with "ten thousands (plural) of his holy ones" (Jude 14-15). That phrase "ten thousands" is also translated as "ten million" (1 Enoch 1:9). Yahweh's heavenly chariots at Sinai were "twice ten thousand, thousands upon thousands" (Psalm 68:17). In Daniel's vision of heavenly host before Yahweh's throne, he sees "a thousand thousands served him, and ten thousand times ten thousand (one hundred million) stood before him" (Daniel 7:10). Jeremiah comes right out and says, "The host of heaven cannot be numbered" (Jeremiah 33:22).

Shining Ones and Stars

One more thing about this heavenly host. They are sometimes described as "shining." For example, in Daniel's vision on the Tigris River, he sees an unnamed heavenly warrior speaking of the various territorial principalities over the nations called "princes" or guardians of those lands (10:12-13, 20-21). The heavenly being is described as a man whose "body was like beryl [a gleaming gem], his face like the appearance of lightning, his eyes like flaming torches, his arms and legs like the gleam of burnished bronze" (10:6).

Heavenly creatures are often described in these shining terms in Scripture. Ezekiel's vision of the Cherubim also describe them as "gleaming beryl," glowing "burnished bronze," "gleaming metal," with "bright fire," "flashes of lightning and fire" around them (Ezekiel 1:4-16). Yahweh on his throne is described as the form of a man whose upper half was like "gleaming metal, like the fire enclosed all around," and "there was brightness all around him" (1:26-28).

At Mount Sinai, Yahweh and his host are both described in these terms of shining:

> Deuteronomy 33:2
> He said, "The LORD came from Sinai and dawned from Seir upon us; he shone forth from Mount Paran; he came from the ten thousands of holy ones, with flaming fire at his right hand.

In the New Testament, the angels who announced the resurrection of Jesus had "the appearance like lightning," and clothing "white as snow" (Matthew 28:3), described by Luke as "dazzling in apparel" (Luke 24:4). That was no designer clothes with bling, that was a shining brightness expressive of the heavenly realm.

In fact, even Moses began to shine with an unbearable brightness the more he was in Yahweh's presence in the tabernacle (Exodus 34:29-35).

Isaiah 14 gives a prophecy to the king of Babylon that many believe also refers to the satan. Yahweh taunts the human king who considered himself to be divine with intent to ascend above the very throne of God, "How you are fallen from heaven, O Day Star, son of Dawn!" (14:12). The first part of that name, "Day Star," is *helel* in Hebrew, which lexicons define as meaning "Shining One."[8] We will talk more about this passage in a second, but the context of it is clearly one of spiritual or heavenly connection. In his arrogant pride, the king of Babylon claims to be divine, like the shining beings of the heavenly host.

---

[8] "Shining one" Francis Brown, Samuel Rolles Driver, and Charles Augustus Briggs, *Enhanced Brown-Driver-Briggs Hebrew and English Lexicon* (Oxford: Clarendon Press, 1977), 237.

This "shining" was a well-known rendering of spiritual beings through all the ancient world. A fragment of the Dead Sea Scrolls speaks of "those who make knowledge shine among the divinities [gods] of light." [9] The Canaanite religious texts from Ugarit in Syria describe the same kind of divine council of gods around their supreme god, El. They are called, "the Shining Ones of the council." [10] As far away as ancient China, we find references to a supreme creator, Shang Di, also surrounded by lesser deities or spirits called, *shen*, which means, "bright ones." [11]

And in the popular Egyptian Book of the Dead, the deified dead scribe, now called Osiris Ani, speaks of the gods also as "Shining Ones" who "live in the rays of light," as emanations of the sun god Ra. [12]

> I may lift up the earth; that the shining ones may open their arms unto me; that the company of the gods may speak with the words of the shining ones unto Osiris Ani; that the hearts of the gods may direct [him]; and that they may make him powerful in heaven among the gods who have taken unto themselves visible forms. [13]

So, why all this brightness and shining of the gods? Is it just a manifestation of spiritual glory or is there more to it than that?

A closer look reveals that the shining of heavenly host reflects a strong literary and theological identification of the gods with stars. Some passages appear to address the "host of heaven" as the stars in the sky; and other passages appear to address the "host of heaven" as the spiritual beings around God's throne. This is because the stars and gods

---

[9] 4Q403 1.2.35 - Florentino García Martínez and Eibert J. C. Tigchelaar, *"The Dead Sea Scrolls Study Edition (translations)"* (Leiden; New York: Brill, 1997–1998), 823.

[10] E. Theodore Mullen, Jr., *The Divine Council in Canaanite and Early Hebrew Literature* (Chico, CA: Scholars Press, 1980), 240.

[11] John Ross, *The Original Religion of China*, (New York, NY: Eaton and Mains, 1909), 172.

[12] Book of the Dead LXXVIII (78). E. Wallis Budge, *The Egyptian Book of the Dead: The Papyrus of Ani* (1895), 333.

[13] Book of the Dead CXXIV (174:10-12). Budge, *The Egyptian Book of the Dead*, 331. Pharaoh Pepi was also deified and described as standing "among the gods, among the shining ones." Budge, *The Egyptian Book of the Dead*, 57-58

were thought of as interchangeable in their identities. Stars were equated with gods and gods were equated with stars. This explains the development of astrology as the stars determining our destiny: because the ancient mind thought of the stars as gods and the gods controlled their lives. So then, the stars controlled their lives because they were manifestations of the gods.

When Moses warned the Israelites of worshipping the Canaanite deities, he likened the sun, moon and stars to "all the host of heaven."

> Deuteronomy 4:19-20
> And beware lest you raise your eyes to heaven, and when you see the sun and the moon and the stars, all the host of heaven, you be drawn away and bow down to them and serve them, things that the LORD your God has allotted to all the peoples under the whole heaven. But the LORD has taken [Israel] and brought you out of the iron furnace, out of Egypt, to be a people of his own inheritance, as you are this day.

On the surface, this looks like he is saying that the pagans worship the sun, moon and stars as deities. That is true. But not true enough. Notice the language that Yahweh has "allotted" those host to the peoples under heaven, while keeping Israel as his own "inheritance." This phrase and terminology is repeated with the same juxtaposition of Israel and the peoples later in Deuteronomy 32.

> Deuteronomy 32:8–9
> When the Most High gave to the nations their
>   inheritance,
>   when he divided mankind,
> he fixed the borders of the peoples
>   according to the number of the sons of God.
> But the LORD's portion is his people,
>   Jacob his allotted heritage.

In both Deuteronomy 4 and 32, we see the same repeated pattern of God allotting the peoples (nations) to the Sons of God—who are the host of heaven—as an inheritance, but keeping Israel (Jacob) as his own allotted inheritance. Earlier, we found that the Sons of God were in fact the divine beings around Yahweh's throne (who had rebelled). So we see that the Sons of God are equated with the host of heaven as both gods and as astronomical bodies. It is a case of both/and, not either/or. The Sons of God are the heavenly host, which is both a personal divine being from God's throne, and represented in the sun, moon and stars that were worshipped by pagans.

The Jews also equated the heavenly host as both stars and gods, but they refused to worship them. And remember, the phrase, "gods" in Hebrew was *elohim*, which was synonymous with the Sons of God in Yahweh's divine council (Psalm 82:1 with Job 1:6). Thus, Job ties the two together when he describes the Sons of God as "morning stars" singing together at God's creation of the universe.

> Job 38:7
> when the <u>morning stars</u> sang together and all the <u>sons</u>
> <u>of God</u> shouted for joy.

This verse uses a very common technique called "parallelism" that is ubiquitous in the Old Testament. Parallelism uses a doublet of phrases to convey the same thing in two different ways. "Morning stars singing" is another way of saying "sons of God shouting for joy." They are not two different things, but the same thing repeated with different words. The conjunctive "and" in Hebrew means "even" in this context. So, the text is not saying morningstars *and* all the sons of God, as if they are two different items, but rather, "morningstars, *even* all the sons of God."

Daniel also uses this parallel doublet in a passage identifying spiritual principalities with stars. Notice the conjunctive *and* again as meaning *even*.

Dan. 8:10-11

"It grew great, even to the host of heaven. And some of the host **and** some of the stars it threw down to the ground and trampled on them. It became great, even as great as the Prince of the host [Michael]"

The spiritual "princes" over the nations in this passage are also called "host of heaven" and "stars."

This poetic technique now makes more sense of Psalm 148:

Psalm 148:2–3
Praise him, all his angels;
    praise him, all his hosts!
Praise him, sun and moon,
    praise him, all you shining stars!

This Psalm also uses parallel doublets as well. Its call to praise is not a listing of separate things created by God: angels, hosts, sun and moon, shining stars; it is a parallel synonym of angels, who are his hosts, which are also his shining stars!

Now, remember that prophecy of Isaiah to the king of Babylon we brought up earlier in this chapter? That "Day Star, Son of the Dawn" in Hebrew is *Helel ben Shachar* which literally means "shining one, son of the dawn," and is actually a well known ancient reference to the planet Venus, known to the ancients as the "bright morning star."[14] The shining of astronomical bodies was the same shining of the divine Sons of God/gods/Watchers.

As I explained in more detail in my previous book, When Giants Were Upon the Earth, this Isaiah passage is not really about "Satan's fall from heaven," but rather a mockery of the king of Babylon's fall from earthly power by placing him into a retelling of a Canaanite myth of the god

---

[14] Michael S. Heiser, *The Unseen Realm: Recovering the Supernatural Worldview of the Bible*, First Edition (Bellingham, WA: Lexham Press, 2015), 85

Athtar's own failed ambitions. The king thought he would be like a god, but he will end up dead and in Sheol like every rebel.

Isaiah 14:3, 12–15

You will take up this taunt against the king of Babylon:
"How you are fallen from heaven,
    O Day Star, son of Dawn!
How you are cut down to the ground,
    you who laid the nations low!
You said in your heart,
    'I will ascend to heaven;
above the stars of God
    I will set my throne on high;
I will sit on the mount of assembly
    in the far reaches of the north;
I will ascend above the heights of the clouds;
    I will make myself like the Most High.'
But you are brought down to Sheol,
    to the far reaches of the pit

Scholar Michael S. Heiser definitively explains the linguistic and narrative referent of Helel ben Shachar (Day Star, son of the Dawn) as being the Ugaritic god Athtar from the epic Baal Cycle of myths at Ugarit. Heiser reveals that Athtar was equated with the planet Venus. Athtar sought to raise himself above "the stars of El," (gods as stars, again) a reference to the divine council or heavenly host that surrounded the high god of the Canaanite pantheon. He tried to do so by seeking to sit on the throne of Baal, referred to as "the Most High," upon the "mount of assembly" in the north called Saphon—just like in the prophecy of Isaiah. But Athtar was not powerful enough for the position of power and was cast to earth/Sheol.[15]

[15] Michael Heiser, "The Mythological Provenance of Isaiah 14:12-15: A Reconsideration of the Ugaritic Material" Liberty University https://digitalcommons.liberty.edu/lts_fac_pubs/280/

In the New Testament, Jude writes about another fall of divine beings in the days of the Flood, "angels who did not keep their own domain, but abandoned their proper abode" and fell to earth. God then imprisoned them "in eternal chains under gloomy darkness until the judgment of the great day" (Jude 6). Jude calls these imprisoned fallen angels "wandering stars" (v. 13), in line with Enoch's "prison house for the stars and the powers of heaven... they are the ones which have transgressed the commandments of God" (1Enoch 18:14-15).[16]

This astralization of deities now brings some clarification to the poetic imagery used in many biblical prophesies of a collapsing universe. Falling stars, darkening suns, blood red moons and skies rolling up like a scroll are not scientific descriptions of the physical universe crumbling, they are a common mythopoeic image of heavenly rulers (Watchers) falling from power along with their earthly kingly counterparts. We saw previously in this chapter that the ancient Hebrew mind conceived of the earthly authorities as linked with their heavenly principalities. So then, Yahweh's judgment upon earthly powers and their heavenly counterparts is described as the astronomical heavens crashing down in defeat.

Here is a list of some passages that use astronomical catastrophe as symbol of spiritual and earthly powers at war:

• Judges 5:19-20 – kings of Canaan fighting on earth are described as "stars fighting from heaven."

• Isaiah 13:1-17 – the fall of Babylon to the Medes in 539 B.C. described as stars of heaven and the constellations not flashing forth their light, the sun darkened and the moon not shedding light.

• Haggai 2:6 – the promise of a New Covenant described as "shaking the heavens and earth." (See with this, Hebrews 12:26-28)

---

[16] James H. Charlesworth, The Old Testament Pseudepigrapha, vol. 1 (New York; London: Yale University Press, 1983), 23.

• Amos 8:9 – the fall of Samaria in 722 B.C. described as the sun going down at noon and the earth dark in broad daylight.

• Isaiah 30:25-26 – Israel's defeat of Sennacherib in 701 B.C. described as the moon being as a bright as the sun and the sun seven times brighter.

• Psalm 18:6-15 – David's deliverance from Saul described as earth reeling, mountains quaking heavens coming down with thick darkness, and the foundations of the earth laid bare.

• Joel 2:30–31 – Wonders in the heavens, the sun turning to darkness and the moon turning to blood are all described by the apostle Peter as being fulfilled in the first century in the fall of Israel and Jerusalem to the power of Rome (Acts 2:16, 20-21).

Centuries after Moses, in the 6th century B.C., Yahweh would destroy Egypt "by the hand of Nebuchadnezzar king of Babylon" (Ezekiel 30:10-11). Pagan Babylon would be a weapon of judgment in Yahweh's hand. Yahweh describes the judgment poetically, "I will dry up the Nile…I will bring desolation upon the land" (Ezekiel 30:12). Drying up the Nile was an obvious figurative image of "drying up" Egypt's wealth, since the river was the essence of her wealth (v. 10) The Nile never literally dried up. Then he gives this revealing description of astronomical catastrophe:

> Ezekiel 32:7–8
> When I blot you out, I will cover the heavens and make
> their stars dark; I will cover the sun with a cloud, and
> the moon shall not give its light. All the bright lights of
> heaven will I make dark over you, and put darkness on
> your land, declares the Lord GOD.

This destruction occurred around 580 B.C. But we have no records of these astronomical events occurring along with the historical ones. While these descriptions are certainly possible as physical phenomena, they are not necessarily so, because as I've noted elsewhere, the entire Exodus story is framed as a war of Yahweh on Pharaoh and the gods of Egypt. So whether this is literal or not, the meaning is certainly that Yahweh would "put the lights out" of both earthly Egypt and her heavenly principalities that ruled over her.

But there are many other examples of this astronomical language that is clearly not literal astronomical phenomena, but metaphorical reference to the fall of powers. Many of them refer to the same Babylonian campaign of conquest in the same time period.

When Babylon invaded Judah in 587 B.C., it also took out Edom. And the prophet Isaiah predicted that fall of kingdoms as "All the host of heaven shall rot away, and the skies roll up like a scroll. All their host shall fall, as leaves fall from the vine, like leaves falling from the fig tree." (Isaiah 34:4).

Edom fell in the 6th century B.C., but these astronomical events never occurred, because of course, if the sky rolled up like that and all the stars fell, we wouldn't be here. There would be no universe left. That could not possibly be literal. It was the description, not of physical phenomena, but spiritual events of earthly and heavenly powers being overthrown.

And when that same Babylon destroyed Israel and led her into captivity in that same time period, the same prophet Isaiah predicted it in vivid poetic language as the "earth will be completely laid waste and despoiled" (Isaiah 24:3), the earth is "split and broken asunder" (24:19), something that could not and did not happen physically or scientifically, but was symbolic. And then Isaiah says that in this event of judgment, God will simultaneously punish the earthly rulers together with their heavenly counterparts, the "host of heaven," or the Watchers, principalities of power over the peoples.

41

Isaiah 24:21–23
On that day the LORD will punish <u>the host of heaven, in
heaven, and the kings of the earth, on the earth</u>. They
will be gathered together as <u>prisoners in a pit</u>; they will
be shut up in a prison, and after many days they will be
punished. Then <u>the moon will be confounded and the
sun ashamed</u>.

The "confounding" of the moon and "shaming" of the sun is a poetic way
of saying the principalities and powers will be humbled by their defeat.
One cannot confound the physical moon or shame the physical sun.

One last example gives this notion of astronomical catastrophe a clear
metaphorical reference to the spiritual realm. When Babylon ended up
destroying Jerusalem and the temple in its 6th century campaign of
conquest, Jeremiah the prophet described it as if the entire world was
being returned to a pre-creation state of chaos. The very spiritual cosmos
of the covenant as incarnate in the temple was being undone. Jeremiah
uses the creation language of Genesis 1 but retells it as if creation is being
undone. Chaos is overtaking the order established by God.

Jeremiah 4:23–28
I looked on the earth, and behold, it was <u>without form
and void;</u>
and to the <u>heavens, and they had no light</u>.
I looked on the <u>mountains,</u> and behold, they were
<u>quaking,</u>
and all the <u>hills moved to and fro</u>.
I looked, and behold, there <u>was no man,</u>
and all the <u>birds of the air had fled</u>.
I looked, and behold, the fruitful <u>land was a desert,</u>
and all its cities were laid in ruins
before the LORD, before his fierce anger.

For thus says the LORD, "The <u>whole land shall be a</u>
   <u>desolation; yet</u>
   <u>I will not make a full end</u>.
"For this the <u>earth shall mourn</u>,
   and the <u>heavens above be dark</u>."

The language should tip off the reader that this is a symbolic literary connection to Genesis 1. He says the earth "was without form and void," the exact same Hebrew words of Genesis 1:1 that described the chaos before God started creating. This obviously is not literal but symbolic, because the earth was not physically returned to that chaos state in 586 B.C. It is a statement of spiritual chaos, not literal physical destruction of the earth.

Then Jeremiah describes a kind of emptying of the things of heaven and earth created in the six days. No more birds in the air undoes the creation on the fifth day. No more vegetation on the earth is an undoing of the third day of creation. The elimination of all humans ("no man") is the elimination of the sixth day of creation. Obviously all the humans on earth were not killed in 586 B.C. The heavens going dark is a description of the spiritual realm being emptied of the power and influence they were created with on the fourth day. The heavens going dark is an undoing of the first act of creation and a return to the primeval darkness. Astronomical catastrophe was a metaphor to describe the fall or judgment of both earthly powers and their spiritual principalities, the heavenly host.

For more in depth study of the language of cosmic collapse in biblical prophecy, see my book <u>End Times Bible Prophecy: It's Not What They Told You</u> (affiliate link).

But what of the judgment of these rebellious Watchers in Psalm 82? What is it and when does it occur?

Chapter 3:
The Judgment of the Watchers

In chapters 1 and 2, I examined Psalm 82 to discover that it talks about God having a heavenly host of divine beings around his throne that counsel with him and carry out his judgments or decisions. They are called "holy ones" (Deut 33:2-3; Jude 14), "heavenly host" (1King 22:19) "the divine council" (Psa 82:1), and "Sons of God" (Job 5:1; 15:15).

Then I showed how God had separated the seventy Gentile nations at Babel, placing them under the authority of fallen Sons of God, now also called Watchers (Dan 4:13, 17), who were supposed to rule with justice, but instead ruled unjustly and in darkness. This resulted in their punishment.

But what kind of punishment is it and when does it occur?

Like Men You Shall Die

I believe the Watcher's punishment is loss of both their immortality and their inheritance of nations at Babel. And I will argue that this was accomplished in the first-century complex of events of Messiah's death, resurrection, ascension and arrival of God's kingdom. Let's take another look at Psalm 82 to get a good reminder of the narrative.

> Psalm 82:6–8
> I said, "You are gods,
>   sons of the Most High, all of you;
> nevertheless, like men you shall die,
>   and fall like any prince."

> Arise, O God, judge the earth;
> for you shall inherit all the nations!

The first aspect of God's judgment upon the gods of the nations is in verses 6 and 7. Apparently, their punishment is the loss of immortality, resulting in death like mortal humans. Though they were gods with divine immortality, they will now die like men.

The question is, what is this death? Is it literal or metaphorical? If it is literal, then the text indicates that the immortal Watchers would lose their immortality and die just like earthly princes. It seems to be a humiliation of the heavenly princes who would otherwise survive their earthly princes' demise. But in this case, the gods are being stripped of their immortality and, thus, their divinity. Death does not become divine beings. So death would be a most serious punishment for such a creature.

Isaiah confirms this loss of immortality when he describes the day of the Watchers' judgment:

> Isaiah 24:21–22
> On that day the LORD will punish the host of heaven, in heaven, and the kings of the earth, on the earth. They will be gathered together as prisoners in a pit; they will be shut up in a prison, and after many days they will be punished.

Notice how the fate of the Watchers is tied to the fate of their allotted nations. The divine host of heaven will die together with their earthly kings or princes. And death is described here in the common Old Testament image of "the pit" of Sheol or Hades, the underworld of the dead (Isa 38:18; Ezek 31:16; Pss 30:3; 88:3–4; Prov 1:12), followed by some kind of punishment.

The New Testament confirms this death of the Watchers that it calls the "rulers of this age" who are "doomed to pass away."

1 Corinthians 2:6
Yet among the mature we do impart wisdom, although
it is not a wisdom of this age or of the rulers of this age,
who are doomed to pass away.

I will explain in Chapter 4 that these rulers are not merely earthly rulers, but the spiritual rulers over those earthly ones; and then in Chapter 5 that their passing away will be at the end of the age. But for now, I just wanted to address the "doom of passing away" as being a reference to the death or loss of immortality in Psalm 82. The Greek root word translated as "doomed to pass away" in this 1 Corinthians verse (*katargeo*) is the same root as that used later by Paul of the destruction of every ruler and authority and even of death itself at the end.

1 Corinthians 15:24–26
Then comes the end, when [Jesus] delivers the
kingdom to God the Father after destroying (*katargeo*)
every rule and every authority and power. For he must
reign until he has put all his enemies under his feet.
The last enemy to be destroyed (*katargeo*) is death.

Katargeo is defined in lexicons as meaning "to destroy or render powerless."[17] So the fate of the ruling Watchers will be the same fate as that of death itself, namely destruction and powerlessness. But of what does this destruction, this death, this doom and punishment consist? Is it mere loss of authority, or do they actually die like human princes? Do they simply cease to exist? It is at this point that the lack of detail in the biblical text tempts us to consider texts that are outside the canon— though considered worthy by the canon—to answer the question.

The biblical source material of 1 Enoch suggests some detail that may shed light on the ancient Judeo-Christian understanding of the fate of the Watchers. As I have argued in a booklet on the book of 1 Enoch, the

---

[17] Horst Robert Balz and Gerhard Schneider, *Exegetical Dictionary of the New Testament* (Grand Rapids, Mich.: Eerdmans, 1990–), 267.

New Testament has drawn much from this pseudepigraphal text regarding the Watchers of the ancient world.

Jude paraphrases the storyline of 1 Enoch and then quotes verse 1:9 to describe God's coming judgment:

> Jude 14–15
> It was also about these that Enoch, the seventh from Adam, prophesied, saying, "Behold, the Lord comes with ten thousands of his holy ones, to execute judgment on all and to convict all the ungodly of all their deeds of ungodliness that they have committed in such an ungodly way, and of all the harsh things that ungodly sinners have spoken against him." [This is quoted from 1 Enoch 1:9]

Jude 6-7 and 1 Peter 3:18 draw from 1 Enoch to describe the sin of the Watchers before the Flood and their punishment of being chained in Tartarus "until the judgment of the great day."[18] One need not require acceptance of 1 Enoch as Scriptural canon to affirm its story of the Watchers as having some truth. After all, the New Testament authors do. How much of 1 Enoch is true is certainly up for debate, but it is a biblically legitimate resource for seeking some answers.

For a detailed argument of Evangelical Christian respect for the book of 1 Enoch, see my booklet on 1 Enoch.

The Judgment of Fire

1 Enoch 10 describes the fate of the pre-Flood heavenly Watchers who defied God by fornicating with earthly women. They are first bound

---

[18] Lest anyone misunderstand Jude's reference to the location of the binding of the angels, Peter locates it right in Sheol, as Enoch did. He writes that God "did not spare the angels when they sinned, but cast them into hell and committed them to chains of gloomy darkness" (v. 4). The word for "hell" in this passage is not gehenna, the traditional designation for the English translation of hell. Tartaroo is a Greek word that refers to Tartarus, the deepest location in Sheol, where it was said in Greek lore that the gigantic Titans were chained. Enoch however says this is where the fallen angels, the Watchers, were chained (1 En. 63:10-64:1).

beneath the rocks of the earth to await their judgment. And what is that judgment? Death. Just like the punishment explained for the post-Babel Watchers in Psalm 82:7. Then that "death judgment" is further unpacked as involving burning destruction. Here is the actual text:

> 1 Enoch 10:11-15
> And to Michael God said, "Make known to Semyaza and the others who are with him, who fornicated with the women, that they will die together with them in all their defilement. And when they and all their children have battled with each other, and when they have seen the destruction of their beloved ones, bind them for seventy generations underneath the rocks of the ground until the day of their judgment and of their consummation, until the eternal judgment is concluded. In those days they will lead them into the bottom of the fire—and in torment—in the prison (where) they will be locked up forever. And at the time when they will burn and die, those who collaborated with them will be bound together with them from henceforth unto the end of (all) generations. And destroy all the souls of pleasure and the children of the Watchers, for they have done injustice to man.[19]

These pre-Flood Watchers who fornicated with human women are not the same persons as the post-Babel Watchers who were allotted the nations, but their judgment of "death" is the same: the loss of their immortality through death. It is likely that the death in Psalm 82 involves the same fire as in 1 Enoch 10. And that fire is later described as the "furnace of fire."

> 1 Enoch 54:6
> Then Michael, Raphael, Gabriel, and Phanuel themselves shall seize [the sinful Watchers] on that

---

[19] James H. Charlesworth, *The Old Testament Pseudepigrapha*, vol. 1 (New York; London: Yale University Press, 1983), 18.

great day of judgment and cast them into the furnace
(of fire) that is burning that day, so that the Lord of the
Spirits may take vengeance on them.[20]

Whether the "furnace of fire" is literal or not, it certainly pictures God's final judgment of destruction for those beings. This imagery of a fiery furnace of judgment is also used by Jesus in his parables when he describes the judgment of all sinners and law-breakers at the end of the age.

> Matthew 13:41–42
> The Son of Man will send his angels, and they will
> gather out of his kingdom all causes of sin and all law-
> breakers, and throw them into the fiery furnace. In that
> place there will be weeping and gnashing of teeth. (see
> also Matt 13:49-50)

Though the Matthean parable seems to be referring to human sinners, it is not too much of a stretch to conclude that law-breaking angels who cause sin will be included in that fiery judgment, especially since 1 Enoch describes a furnace of fire for the Watchers as well.

The book of Revelation describes a "lake of fire" where the beast, the false prophet, the devil, Death and Hades, and indeed, all unbelieving sinners will have their end (Rev 20:10, 15; 21:8). Is this lake of fire the same furnace of fire that Enoch and Jesus taught about? The similarities and connections are too strong to deny. They are both used to describe the punishment of sinful humans and Watchers in fire. And they both occur at the same time, the "end of the age," the "day of judgment."

Is it too speculative to posit that rebellious post-Babel Watchers over the nations would die the same death that involves the same judgment in the same lake (or furnace) of fire as rebellious pre-Flood Watchers and other spiritual and human sinners? Perhaps, but it seems far more speculative to suggest otherwise.

---

[20] James H. Charlesworth, *The Old Testament Pseudepigrapha,* vol. 1 (New York; London: Yale University Press, 1983), 38.

Revelation 20:15; 21:8
And if anyone's name was not found written in the
book of life, he was thrown into the lake of fire...But
as for the cowardly, the faithless, the detestable, as for
murderers, the sexually immoral, sorcerers, idolaters,
and all liars, their portion will be in the lake that burns
with fire and sulfur, which is the second death."

Remember, Jesus himself said that the eternal fire (another synonym for
Lake of Fire) was actually made "for the devil and his angels" (Matt
25:41). So eternal fire once again appears to be the final judgment for
fallen angels or Watchers.

Stoicheia: The Elemental Spirits

I believe there is another possible hint at the fiery destruction of the
Watchers in 2 Peter 3. The relevant passage reads,

2 Peter 3:10-12
But the day of the Lord will come like a thief, and then
the heavens will pass away with a roar, and the
heavenly bodies will be burned up and dissolved...
waiting for and hastening the coming of the day of
God, because of which the heavens will be set on fire
and dissolved, and the heavenly bodies will melt as
they burn!

In this passage that refers to the judgment of the last days (2 Pet 3:3), I
want to focus on the word "heavenly bodies." In Greek, that word is
stoicheia. Though some believe *stoicheia* is a reference to astronomical
bodies like the sun, moon and stars, others believe it is better translated
as "elements," such as the periodic table of the material universe. But
these are both physical interpretations that reflect our modern scientific
materialist bias.

There is another scholarly interpretation that argues for a spiritual interpretation of *stoicheia* in this passage. It is only used five other times in the New Testament. In three of those places, the context seems to refer to the "elementary principles" of the old covenant (Gal 4:3, 9; Heb 5:12). These have nothing to do with the physical periodic table of elements or astronomical bodies.

> Hebrews 5:12
> For though by this time you ought to be teachers, you need someone to teach you again the basic principles [*stoicheia*] of the oracles of God...

In the two other places *stoicheia* occurs (Col 2:8, 20), it is used in reference to the elementary principles of pagan worldviews.

> Colossians 2:8
> See to it that no one takes you captive by philosophy and empty deceit, according to human tradition, according to the elemental spirits [*stoicheia*] of the world, and not according to Christ.

But it is here that there is some ambiguity. Some translations render *stoicheia* here as "elemental spirits," because there is reason to believe the term is a spiritual one that refers to the bondage of the nations to the spiritual powers.[21] This would be consistent with the Deuteronomy 32 worldview of the Gentile nations under the Watchers' authority.

---

[21] "We may consider the suggestion that stoicheia tou kosmou was Paul's particular way of referring to "local presiding deities" or "national 'gods' " who rule over territories and races. N. T. Wright has argued for this meaning in Colossians, understanding Paul to be engaged in a polemic against Judaism rather than some sort of Jewish-Hellenistic syncretism, and he sees the same meaning operative in Galatians (see Wright, 101–2, 115–16). Following and developing this line of interpretation we could understand ta stoicheia tou kosmou as a broad, inclusive term that embraced the whole host of spiritual beings known individually as principalities, powers, dominions and rulers, the equivalent to the angels or gods of the nations (see Principalities and Powers). In Galatians 4:8 Paul speaks of the Galatians as formerly enslaved to "those beings which by nature are no gods." This analysis of the Galatian Gentiles' former situation resonates with the Jewish notion that the gods of the nations are not really what they appear to be; they are but spiritual powers appointed as national guardians by Yahweh, ultimately subservient to him alone, but falsely regarded as "gods" by the nations." Gerald F. Hawthorne, Ralph P. Martin, and Daniel G. Reid, eds., *Dictionary of Paul and His Letters* (Downers Grove, IL: InterVarsity Press, 1993), 232.

If this interpretation of *stoichea* is applied to 2 Peter 3:10-12, then what we see is a picture perfectly consistent with Psalm 82, 1 Enoch, Matthew and Revelation as described above. At the Day of the Lord, God will judge and burn up with fire those spiritual powers, the Watchers, who ruled unjustly over the nations along with their human equivalents.

But one question remains: When does this judgment of the Watchers' death take place? When are they thrown into the lake of fire? 1 Enoch says after seventy generations from the Flood. The New Testament says at the end of the age. But when is that? Is it in our future? Or did it already happen? The answer might shock you.

Chapter 4:
The Inheritance of the Nations

In previous chapters, I unpacked Psalm 82 to show that it talks about God having a heavenly host of divine beings around his throne. Some of these beings, called Watchers, were given the Gentile nations as an allotted inheritance in contrast with Israel as God's inheritance. But those heavenly host ruled their nations unjustly. This resulted in their punishment of death like humans, and most likely destruction in the lake of fire.

It is now the question of *when* this judgment of the Watchers occurs that I want to address. Many would assume it occurs at the end of the world in our future. But I think the text of Psalm 82 implies that it has already happened in our past.

Here is the relevant text of the Psalm to look at again:

> Psalm 82:5–8
> They have neither knowledge nor understanding,
>> they walk about in darkness;
>> all the foundations of the earth are shaken.
>
> I said, "You are gods,
>> sons of the Most High, all of you;
> nevertheless, like men you shall die,
>> and fall like any prince."
> Arise, O God, judge the earth;
>> for you shall inherit all the nations!

The Foundations of the Earth are Shaken

There are three reasons in the Psalm that make me conclude that the capital punishment of the fallen Watchers occurred in the first century AD in conjunction with the coming of Messiah. 1) Verse 5 refers to "the foundations of the earth" being shaken. This is a reference to the consummation of the new covenant that came in Christ to overturn the Deuteronomic inheritance. 2) Verse 8 sets the context of the judgment at the resurrection of Messiah, which resulted in 3) Messiah's subsequent inheritance of the nations in the first century.

Let me explain each one.

First, the phrase "all the foundations of the earth are shaken" (v. 5) ties the context of the Watchers' judgment to the arrival of the new covenant. The concept of the shaking of heavens and earth is a common notion in the Old and New Testaments. It is used figuratively to describe the spiritual reality of an earthly event.

In Haggai 2:21-22, the prophet is told to tell the governor of Judah that God is going to "shake the heavens and the earth, and to overthrow the throne of kingdoms. I am about to destroy the strength of the kingdoms of the nations." This prophecy explains the shaking of heavens and earth as a symbolic reference to the destruction of the strength of kingdoms.

Shaking heavens and earth is commonly used as a metaphor for God overthrowing kingdoms or establishing a new authority (Isa 40:3-5; Hab 3:6-7, 9-10; Micah 1:3-7; Jer 4:23-30; Nahum 1:4-6; Psa 18:6-15; Judges 5:4-5).

The New Testament uses the imagery of shaking the heavens and earth as an expression of the spiritual impact of covenants. John the Baptizer's proclamation was described as a leveling of mountains and upheaval of valleys.

Luke 3:3–6
[John the Baptizer] went into all the region around the
Jordan, proclaiming a baptism of repentance for the
forgiveness of sins. As it is written in the book of the
words of Isaiah the prophet, "The voice of one crying in
the wilderness: 'Prepare the way of the Lord, make his
paths straight. Every valley shall be filled, and every
mountain and hill shall be made low, and the crooked
shall become straight, and the rough places shall become
level ways, ⁶ and all flesh shall see the salvation of God.'"

This cosmic geological eruption occurred in the first century with the
coming of Messiah. John the Baptizer was not pronouncing the second
coming of Christ, he was pronouncing the first coming of Christ. So the
terminology of the earth shaking was a spiritual reference to the impact
of the New Covenant arrival. God becoming flesh in the savior Jesus is
described as "all flesh seeing the salvation of God." That's obviously
hyperbole. It was not literally physical as many Christians often
mistakenly interpret prophecy. Why? Because it was a metaphor for the
historic change of covenants and earthly powers.

In Hebrews 12, the creation of the old Mosaic covenant is described
figuratively as God "shaking the earth," with the institution of his
world-changing covenant. The new covenant in Christ is then referred
to as a final shaking of the heavens and earth. The institution of the new
covenant kingdom of God will never be shaken, that is, never be
changed.

Hebrews 12:26–28
At that time [of the old covenant] his voice shook the
earth, but now he has promised, "Yet once more I will
shake not only the earth but also the heavens." This
phrase, "Yet once more," indicates the removal of
things that are shaken—that is, things that have been
made—in order that the things that cannot be shaken

may remain. Therefore let us be grateful for <u>receiving a kingdom that cannot be shaken</u>.

The arrival of the Mosaic old covenant was described in terms of God shaking the earth (v. 26). This is not a reference to physical earthquakes, but to the spiritual impact of covenant-making. We know this because the new covenant kingdom in Christ is described in like manner as a spiritual shaking of the heavens and earth of the old covenant, to replace it with a superior, permanent new covenant.

So the reference in Psalm 82:5 of God shaking the foundations of the earth is a symbolic reference to the arrival of the new covenant kingdom which is linked to the judgment of the Watchers. When the old covenant is abolished and replaced with the new covenant, God will take back the allotment of authority to the Watchers and judge them.

This connection between Psalm 82 and Hebrews 12 is made all the stronger when one realizes that Hebrews 12 is quoting Haggai 2 that prophesies the new covenant kingdom.

> Haggai 2:6–7
> For thus says the LORD of hosts: Yet once more, in a little while, I will <u>shake the heavens and the earth</u> and the sea and the dry land. And I will <u>shake all nations</u>, so that <u>the treasures of all nations shall come in</u>, and I will fill this house with glory, says the LORD of hosts.

Notice that the last part of that cosmic spiritual shaking of heavens and earth includes the drawing of the nations, the Gentiles, into God's house. The new covenant would involve the messianic inclusion of the Gentiles into the very house of God. That means that the allotted inheritance of the Gentiles to the Sons of God would be taken back by Messiah with the arrival of a new covenant, a new inheritance.

Remember, allotment and inheritance has to do with land and ownership in the old covenant.

That leads us to the next element of our context, the inheritance of the nations.

The Inheritance of the Nations

The last verse of Psalm 82 places the event of the judgment of the Watchers at the time of the inheritance of the nations.

> Psalm 82:8
> Arise, O God, judge the earth;
>   for you shall inherit all the nations!

Before we proceed, it must be noted that the English words that we read as *Gentiles* and *nations* are the same Greek and Hebrew word in the Bible (*ethnos* and *goyim*). "Gentiles" and "nations" are synonyms.

Scripturally, a Gentile was nothing more than a member of one of the seventy nations of Genesis 10 that were allotted to the Watchers in Deuteronomy 32. Sometimes, I will use the words together as "Gentile nations" only to remind the reader of that contextual reality.

This concept of inheriting the nations is messianic. The prophets predicted that when Messiah came, he would not only unite the houses of Judah and Israel, but he would bring the Gentile nations, previously cut off from his covenant, into his new covenant kingdom (Zech 2:6-11; Hos 1:10-11, 2:23; fulfilled in Rom 9:24-29).

At this point, it would be helpful to remember the Deuteronomy 32 worldview with which we started this narrative. God allotted the Gentile nations as an inheritance of the rebellious angelic Sons of God (Deut 32:8-9).

But now in Psalm 2, we read that God will inherit the nations. Or more specifically, Messiah will inherit the nations. God will take away the land deed of the Gentile nations from the Sons of God and give it to Messiah. How do we know this? Because the Psalm says so.

57

Psalm 2:6–8
"As for me, I have set my King on Zion, my holy hill."
I will tell of the decree: The LORD said to me, "You are
my Son; today I have begotten you. Ask of me, and I
will make the nations your heritage, and the ends of the
earth your possession.

Now, some would read this and argue that Jesus becoming king and his
inheritance of the nations may not occur at the same time period in
history. It is possible that he is enthroned as king now, but doesn't
inherit the nations until later in our future. Others think Jesus is not yet
enthroned as king. And both would be wrong.

In Acts 13:32-33, the apostle Paul quotes this same Psalm 2 and
connects it to the resurrection of Jesus.

Acts 13:32–33
"And we bring you the good news that what God
promised to the fathers, this he has fulfilled to us their
children by raising Jesus, as also it is written in the
second Psalm, "'You are my Son, today I have
begotten you.'"

Paul defines the context for Psalm 2 and Messiah's enthronement and
inheritance of the nations *at the time of his resurrection.*

Do you see the powerful imagery here? The resurrection was a kind of
birth from the dead that granted the inheritance of the nations to Jesus
like the birthright of a firstborn son. To confirm this interpretation, Paul
even uses the symbolic phrase "firstborn from the dead" of Jesus in
reference to his resurrection in Colossians 1:18. Firstborn was a legal
term of inheritance. When Jesus resurrected from the dead, he received
the firstborn inheritance.

In Acts 2:30-35, Peter explains that "God had sworn with an oath to him
that he would set one of his descendants on his throne, he foresaw and

spoke about the resurrection of the Christ… being therefore exalted at the right hand of God."

So Christ was enthroned as universal king on heavenly Mount Zion at his resurrection and ascension (Heb 12:22-24). And that throne is over all authority, in heaven and on earth (Eph 1:20-22), including the Watchers and the nations.

At Babel, God gave over the rebellious Gentiles to the false gods they worshipped. He placed them under the authority of the fallen Sons of God. These spiritual princes ruled over their earthly kings and rulers and their fates were intertwined. But the gods of the nations had the title deed to the lands of the nations, and with it, their people.

It is my contention that when Messiah died, resurrected and ascended, he conquered those Watchers and took back the deeds to the nations, which allowed the Gospel of the kingdom to go out into all the world and draw people from every tribe and nation into the new covenant kingdom of God.

To see this narrative, we need to turn to the New Testament affirmation of the Deuteronomy 32 worldview.

New Testament Principalities and Powers

The idea of heavenly principalities over the earthly powers first instituted at Babel and continued on through Daniel is not lost on the New Testament writers.

Paul in particular alludes frequently to the heavenly/earthly connection of principalities and powers.

> Colossians 1:16
> For by him all things were created, in heaven and on earth, visible and invisible, whether thrones or dominions or rulers or authorities…

When Paul tried to encourage the Ephesian Christians suffering persecution from their local authorities, he did so by reminding them that those earthly powers were not the ultimate enemy; the heavenly powers behind them were. Those powers were led by the "prince of the power of the air" Satan (Eph 2:2).

Ephesians 6:12
For we do not wrestle against flesh and blood, but against the rulers, against the authorities, against the cosmic powers over this present darkness, against the spiritual forces of evil in the heavenly places.

But how would these powers be defeated? The secret was rooted in the Gospel that Paul called the "mystery" that God kept from those powers (1 Cor 2:7-8). And guess what that mystery is? The Gospel adoption of Gentile nations into the new covenant kingdom of God through Christ.

Ephesians 3:6
This mystery is that the Gentiles are fellow heirs, members of the same body, and partakers of the promise in Christ Jesus through the gospel.

Remember how those Gentile nations were originally the allotted inheritance of the rebellious Sons of God? Remember how Messiah was promised to one day inherit the nations from those powers? Well, the unity of Gentiles with Jews in the Body of Christ, the Church, is the fulfillment of that messianic inheritance of the nations.

Ephesians 3:10
so that through the church the manifold wisdom of God might now be made known to the rulers and authorities in the heavenly places.

Exactly when did Jesus take back the territorial rights of the nations from the heavenly powers? *At his death, resurrection and ascension into heaven.*

Remember when Jesus told his disciples, after he had risen that "all authority in heaven and on earth has been given to me" (Matt 28:18)? He had *all* authority, not *some* authority. If Watchers still had authority over the nations, then Jesus would not have all authority, and he could not be the Messiah.

Paul links Christ's attainment of all authority to his resurrection and ascension to the right hand of God.

> Ephesians 1:20–22
> that he worked in Christ when he raised him from the dead and seated him at his right hand in the heavenly places, far above all rule and authority and power and dominion, and above every name that is named, not only in this age but also in the one to come. And he put all things under his feet.

So Christ's attainment of authority over all those heavenly powers occurred through his resurrection and ascension. His enthronement constitutes the legal authority taken away from the heavenly powers. The Watchers no longer own their allotted lands of inheritance.

Peter reiterates this submission of all heavenly powers with emphatic clarity.

> 1 Peter 3:22
> [Jesus] has gone into heaven and is at the right hand of God, with angels, authorities, and powers having been subjected to him.

There it is again, Jesus seated at the right hand of God as the ultimate conquest over all heavenly beings. So, all spiritual powers, including the Watchers, were subjected to Christ through his ascension. They simply do not have territorial authority anymore. They simply do not watch over the nations. Jesus Christ watches over the nations. He owns them.

In Chapter 3, I used 1 Corinthians 2:6 as a New Testament expression of the Watchers as heavenly authorities who were "doomed to pass away," or "die like men" (Psalm 82:7).

> 1 Corinthians 2:6–8
> Yet among the mature we do impart wisdom, although it is not a wisdom of this age or of <u>the rulers of this age, who are doomed to pass away</u>. But we impart a secret and hidden wisdom of God, which God decreed before the ages for our glory. <u>None of the rulers of this age understood this, for if they had, they would not have crucified the Lord of glory</u>.

Some might interpret this passage as a reference only to the earthly rulers who crucified Jesus (Acts 4:27-28; 2:23). But it should be clear by now, that Paul's use of the "rulers, authorities and powers" terminology is more in line with the Old Covenant notion of spiritual powers behind the earthly powers. Yes, earthly rulers crucified Jesus, but in truth, they were tools of the spiritual rulers just like the human rulers of Persia and Greece were the tools of the spiritual "princes" of Persia and Greece in Daniel's day (Dan 10:12-13, 20-21). And those spiritual rulers of "this age" were doomed to pass away with the age to come, the age of Messiah. More on that in the next Chapter 5.

Triumphal Procession

But there is more. Paul also reveals the ascension of Christ as involving a violent overthrow of the Watchers. He quotes Isaiah to show that after Christ ascended, he then descended to earth to give spiritual gifts to the Church through the Holy Spirit.

> Ephesians 4:7–10
> But grace was given to each one of us according to the measure of Christ's gift. Therefore it says, "When he ascended on high he led a host of captives, and he gave

gifts to men." (In saying, "He ascended," what does it mean but that he had also descended into the lower regions, the earth?)

Notice that Christ's ascension is described as "leading a host of captives." Some Christians assume these are human captives freed from Hades through Christ's sacrifice. But that is not what the phrase means. It is actually a reference to the common ancient Roman triumphal procession, which involved military victors parading their conquered foes, dead or alive, through the streets of a city. It was rubbing the noses of the vanquished in their defeat and declaring the victor's new authority over those conquered foes.

Scholar Mary Beard describes the ancient Roman Triumph:

> To be awarded a triumph was the most outstanding honor a Roman general could hope for. He would be drawn in a chariot—accompanied by the booty he had won, the prisoners he had taken captive, and his no doubt rowdy and raucous troops in their battle gear—through the streets of the city to the Temple of Jupiter on the Capitoline hill, where he would offer a sacrifice to the god. The ceremony became a by-word for extravagant display...
>
> As the triumphal parade was reaching its last lap, passing through the Forum and about to ascend the Capitoline hill, the prisoners—or at least the most prominent, famous, or dastardly among them—were hauled off for execution and worse, probably in the nearby prison. [22]

Through analogy, Paul is saying that when Christ ascended to his throne at the right hand of God, he led the conquered and captive gods of the nations through spiritual streets as a victorious general and king, and executed them.

---

[22] Mary Beard, *The Roman Triumph* (Mass: Harvard, 2007), 1, 128.

This interpretation is reinforced in Colossians where Paul writes that through the cross Jesus "disarmed the rulers and authorities and put them to open shame, by triumphing over them in him" (Col 2:15).

Beard describes the story from ancient Jewish historian Josephus of the triumph of Vespasian and Titus over Simon bar Gioras that occurred after the Roman destruction of Jerusalem in A.D. 70, the very time period in which Paul wrote his references to Christ's triumph over the powers.

> "Once they had reached the Temple of Jupiter Capitolinus, they stopped. For it was ancestral custom to wait at that point for the announcement of the death of the enemy commander. This was Simon, son of Gioras. He had been led in the procession amongst the prisoners of war; then, a noose round his neck, scourged by his guards, he had been taken to that place next to the Forum where Roman law prescribes that condemned criminals be executed. After the announcement came that he had met his end and the universal cheering that followed it, Vespasian and Titus began the sacrifice."[23]

Beard points out that though there were certainly historical cases of imprisonment in place of execution for the Roman Triumph, its mythology or imagery included execution. This becomes relevant for understanding the proper context of when the Watchers will be judged to "die like men" (Psalm 82:8). The imagery of Triumph in Paul's writing suggests their deaths are tied in with the conclusion of the procession, not in some prophetic future.

Christ's apparent defeat at the cross led to the surprise victory of the resurrection and ascension to universal authority. Captivating, disarming, shaming and triumphing are all violent military words of

---

[23] Beard, *The Roman Triumph*, 129.

subjugation that paint a clear picture of disinherited Watchers who no longer have the power and authority they were once allotted in primeval days. And that defeat includes the imprisonment and execution of the vanquished in the triumphal procession.

That triumphal procession to death is hinted at when Paul uses the same imagery of the Apostles as being led in an earthly Triumph to their deaths.

> 1 Corinthians 4:8-9 (NIV)
> You have begun to reign—and that without us! How I wish that you really had begun to reign so that we also might reign with you! For it seems to me that God has put us apostles on display <u>at the end of the procession, like those condemned to die in the arena</u>. We have been <u>made a spectacle</u> to the whole universe, to angels as well as to human beings.

In this passage, Paul is not referring to the spiritual authorities, but he is using the Triumph imagery again. And notice the reign of new kings follows upon the vanquishing of other authorities, in this case, the apostles! Notice that the assumption is the triumphal procession ends *with the execution of the vanquished in the arena.* "Spectacle" in Greek is the word from which we derive our English word, "theater." To the ancient mind the theater of the procession and arena was symbolic and expressive of the defeat and execution of enemy powers. And the Kingdom of God that Paul was preaching was relevant to both heaven and earth, the heavenly authorities of "angels" as well as the earthly "human beings."

Later, Paul extends the metaphor of Triumph to an ongoing display of the suffering of Christians as a means of converting others.

2 Corinthians 2:14
But thanks be to God, who in Christ always leads us in
triumphal procession, and through us spreads the
fragrance of the knowledge of him everywhere.

Just as the apparent earthly "defeat" of Jesus at the cross would turn around and achieve the real spiritual victory over the powers, so too would the suffering of Christians, and their subjugation to Christ, become an ironic influence on spreading the truth of the Gospel.

There can be no doubt that the principalities and powers, those Sons of God who were allotted the nations at Babel, were finally conquered at the cross and led captive at the ascension of Christ to his enthronement over all powers and authorities in both heaven and earth. But the imagery of Roman Triumph that Paul uses also includes the execution of the "powers and principalities."

Under His Feet

There is another military image that the Scriptures use to describe complete victory over and subjugation of one's enemies, and that is the notion of "placing them under the feet."

A victorious general placing his foot on the necks of the vanquished ruler was a common symbolic activity in the ancient world. Joshua did it to the kings of Canaan when he conquered the Promised Land:

Joshua 10:24–26
Joshua summoned all the men of Israel and said to the
chiefs of the men of war who had gone with him,
"Come near; put your feet on the necks of these kings."
Then they came near and put their feet on their necks.
And Joshua said to them, "Do not be afraid or
dismayed; be strong and courageous. For thus the LORD
will do to all your enemies against whom you fight."

> And afterward Joshua struck them and put them to
> death.

Notice also that the execution of the vanquished was the consummation of that symbolic activity of putting the defeated beneath the victor's feet. This is not a mere symbol of power and authority, it is an incarnation of violent subjugation, followed immediately by execution.

Yet, this is exactly the image used of Christ's victory over the principalities and powers, the Watchers and their minions. As already noted, Ephesians 1:22 says that when Christ was enthroned in heaven, he "put all things under his feet." As a matter of fact, this phrase is part of the most-quoted Old Testament verse in the New Testament, Psalm 110.

> Psalm 110:1
> The LORD says to my Lord: "Sit at my right hand, until
> I put your enemies under your feet."
> (See also Psa 47:2-3; Isa 18:37-38)

Jesus and the apostles affirm that this prophecy of putting enemies under the feet was spoken to the Son of David as part and parcel of his enthronement in heaven, accomplished at his death, resurrection and ascension to the right hand of God (Matt. 22:44; Mark 12:36; Luke 20:42, 43; Acts 2:34, 35).

Now, if you're an informed Bible reader, you will probably be thinking of another connected messianic image that is woven into the tapestry of Scripture. I'm referring to Messiah crushing the head of Satan, the serpent.

In Genesis 3, God curses the serpent because of his deception of Adam and Eve in the Garden. He gives what theologians call the "protoevangelion," the first messianic promise of the Gospel.

Genesis 3:15 (NIV)
And I will put enmity between you [the serpent] and
the woman, and between your offspring and hers; he
will crush your head, and you will strike his heel."

Is this defeat of Satan in our future or in our past or something else?
Later, I will argue that it occurred in our past in the first century (Rom
16:20). For now, just notice that the complex of events of Christ dying,
resurrecting and ascending to his throne is described as a violent
military style subjugation and stripping of authority from spiritual
powers, including the Watchers, a placing of them under his feet,
followed by their execution, and crushing the head of the serpent also
under his feet.

Psalm 82 confirms that connection of the resurrection to the time of
Messiah's inheritance of the nations.

Arise, O God

Psalm 82:8
Arise, O God, judge the earth;
for you shall inherit all the nations!

"Arise, O God..." is on the surface, a call to action for God to stand
from his seated throne of judgment and actively perform his judgments
(Psa 44:26-27; 74:22; 76:9-10).

But I think it goes deeper. I believe that Psalm 82 is referring to the
complex of events surrounding Messiah's death, resurrection and
ascension.

You see, the word for "arise" (*anasta*) in the Greek Old Testament is a
word used of resurrection in the New Testament (Mark 5:41; Acts 9:40;
Eph 5:14). I think Psalm 82 is making a veiled reference to the
resurrection of Messiah as the foundation of the inheritance of the
nations.

But I am not making this symbolic connection from my own poetic imagination; I got it from the apostle Paul. In Romans 15, he writes about Jesus and his resurrection being the catalyst that brings in the Gentiles, as foretold in Isaiah.

> Romans 15:12
> Isaiah says, "The root of Jesse will come, even <u>he who arises to rule the Gentiles;</u> in him will the Gentiles hope."

But when you go back and look at the passage in Isaiah that Paul quotes, we see a slightly different interpretation of the "arising."

> Isaiah 11:10–12
> In that day the root of Jesse, who shall stand as a signal for the peoples—of him shall the [Gentiles] nations inquire, … He will <u>raise a signal</u> for the nations…

Paul quotes the Greek Old Testament here that interpretively changes the raising of a battle standard into the raising of a person. Paul claims that person is Jesus who arose (*anasta*). And it's that same Greek word, *anasta,* that is used in the Greek version of Psalm 82:8 ("Arise, O God").

As New Testament scholars like N.T. Wright point out, the fulfillment of Christ "arising" to rule the nations (Gentiles) is an obvious contextual pointer to Christ's resurrection. So the claim of seeing the resurrection in the statement, "Arise O God, judge the earth. For you shall inherit all the nations (Gentiles)," is not only consistent with apostolic interpretation, it fits the parameters of the new covenant kingdom of Messiah that brings judgment and salvation for all.

The resurrection of Christ permeates Psalm 82. It is the very context that results in and includes Messiah's enthronement as well as his inheritance of the nations.

Some Christians believe that there are still Watchers with territorial control over nations today. That there is still a heavenly "prince of Russia" or "prince of Persia," etc. They justify this by appealing to the fact that many countries are still majority pagan, atheist or Muslim and therefore in bondage to the elemental spirits about which Paul wrote.

But if this is true, it would be equivalent to saying that Jesus did not triumph over the powers at his resurrection (Col 2:15); that he did not lead them captive to imprisonment (Eph 4:8); that Jesus is not enthroned at the right hand of God above all principalities and powers (Eph 1:21); that the Watchers are not under his feet (Eph 1:22); and executed at the conclusion of the triumphal procession (1 Cor 4:8-9); that Messiah did not inherit the nations (Psa 2:6-8); that the Gentiles cannot come into the kingdom because they are still in bondage to those spiritual powers (Rom 15:12); because all these things are tied together as occurring in and through the death, resurrection and ascension of Christ.

The very reason why people from all tribes and peoples and languages are becoming Christians through the Gospel is because Jesus the Messiah has freed them, because Messiah has disinherited the Watchers and has inherited the nations.

Simply stated, the Messiah could not draw people from any of the nations if there were still Watchers with any authority over them. The Watchers were disinherited, judged and died as Psalm 82 predicted; they were disarmed, shamed and triumphed over (Col 2:15), their necks placed under the feet of the conquering Messiah and they were executed. The spiritual authorities were not released to return back to their nations.

But after establishing this narrative of Christus Victor, Christ's victory over the powers, there remains one big glaring issue: If the powers were defeated at the cross, if they were led captive at Christ's ascension, then why did the New Testament describe Christians as still in a wrestling match with them? (Eph 6:12). Does this mean that this struggle with those Watchers over the nations remain for us today? I'll take a look at that next.

Chapter 5:
The End of the Age

I analyzed Psalm 82 to uncover the narrative of Christ's victory over the powers. In it, we saw a reiteration of the Deuteronomy 32 worldview that depicted fallen Sons of God from Yahweh's heavenly host being allotted the Gentile nations as an inheritance, while Yahweh kept Israel for his own inheritance.

These Watchers over the nations were unjust in their governance, so Yahweh declared he would judge them with death through the resurrection of Messiah, which would take back the allotment from the Watchers and give it to Messiah to inherit the nations.

But if Jesus triumphed over the spiritual powers at the cross and then led them captive in a military style triumphal procession, ending in execution, then how is it that the New Testament speaks of an ongoing struggle with those heavenly principalities and powers for the Christian? Are these territorial powers still an issue for us today?

My short answer is that the principalities and powers are not an issue for us today, but they were in Paul's day because when he wrote his New Testament letters, the new covenant had been legally inaugurated at the cross, resurrection and ascension, but was not historically consummated until the destruction of the earthly incarnation of the old covenant, the holy temple in Jerusalem in AD 70. That event was the historical completion of the spiritual truth begun a generation earlier.

Paul was writing in a transition period between covenants. The new had been spiritually inaugurated but not historically consummated until the old had been done away with in the physical world. The old covenant was fading out but had not yet vanished with the destruction of the historical temple (Heb 8:13; 9:8-9).

Thus, the spiritual powers had lost their legal right to the Gentile nations at the complex of events that climaxed with the ascension of Jesus Christ. But their actual judgment of death in the fires of Gehenna took place when the consummation of the inheritance of the nations occurred at the end of the old covenant age.

Many Christians assume that the end of the age or the "last days" is the end of the world. Thus when Jesus speaks of casting sinners into the furnace of fire at the end of the age, they assume this has not yet happened. After all, does not Isaiah place the inheritance of the Gentiles in a future "last days"?

> Isaiah 2:2
> It shall come to pass in the last days that the mountain
> of the house of the LORD shall be established as the
> highest of the mountains, and shall be lifted up above
> the hills; and all the nations shall flow to it...

But I will show that the judgment of the Watchers in Psalm 82 occurred with the inheritance of the Gentiles which actually began in the book of Acts and was completed by AD 70 in the destruction of the temple.

The "last days" occurred in the first century and they were the last days of the old covenant, not the last days of history or the earth. Those last days of the old covenant began with the arrival of Messiah and lasted through the forty years after the cross until the old covenant incarnation, the holy temple, was destroyed in AD 70. So in effect, the forty years from AD 33 or so until AD 70 was a period of transition between covenants, where the new covenant had been inaugurated in the heavenly realm, but not yet consummated in the earthly realm until the earthly incarnation of the old covenant was destroyed. So, in effect, it was an overlap of covenants for forty years.

That's kind of hard for our brains to understand because we want a clean cut break between covenants. But the problem is that God is not a God of mere abstraction and philosophy. He is a God of history. And history is messy. So let me try to help clean up some of the apparent mess.

Acts and the Inheritance of the Gentile Nations

In Acts 2, we read about the first explosion of the Gospel with the first baptism of the Holy Spirit. It was the thing that Jesus had told them to wait for, which would launch them into all the world with the Good News (Acts 1:4).

Pentecost would be the historical inauguration of the heavenly new covenant achieved by the death, resurrection and ascension of Christ. It would be the pouring out of God's Spirit upon his people (Isa 32:12-19; 44:5; Ezek 36:25-28; 37:14).

The disciples asked Jesus if this was the time of the restoration of Israel (1:6). Jesus told them that the regathering or restoration of Israel would begin when the Holy Spirit came upon them soon.

And what was the restoration? The pouring out of God's Spirit and the regathering of Jews from all over the known earth in a metaphorical resurrection (Ezek 37). That's pretty strongly restorative. So when the disciples were baptized with the Spirit at Pentecost and began to speak in foreign tongues, that was the fulfillment of God's pouring out of his Spirit (Acts 2:16-17).

But it was also the beginning of the regathering of Jews because "there were dwelling in Jerusalem Jews, devout men from every nation under heaven" (Acts 2:5). The list of nations that is described (Acts 2:9-11) just happens to be a representative sampling of the seventy nations of Genesis 10, *the very nations that were allotted as an inheritance to the Watchers.*

But those seventy nations were also "all the nations" to which the Jews were scattered (Amos 9:9). And the scattering of the tribes of Israel was described as being swallowed up by the nations (Hosea 8:8). In other words, the tribes of Israel had become so intermingled with the Gentile nations that for Diaspora Jews to return to Jerusalem and follow Messiah constituted the nations being drawn into the new covenant kingdom of God. According to the apostle Luke, Pentecost of AD 30 was not only the ingathering of the tribes of Israel, it was the beginning of the inheritance of the Gentile nations.

Pentecost, AD 30, was the beginning of regathering the scattered Jews AND the reclamation of the divided nations. Pentecost was the undoing of both Exile and Babel.

Scholar Michael Heiser explains this connection of Pentecost to Babel and Exile:

> There are two key terms in [Acts 2] that connect it back to Babel in an unmistakable way. The flaming tongues are described as "divided" (Greek: *diamerizo*), and the crowd, composed of Jews from all the nations, is said to have been "confused" (Greek: *suncheo*).
>
> The second term, *suncheo* (v. 6), is the same word used in the Septuagint version of the Babel story in Genesis 11:7: "Come, let us go down and **confuse** [Septuagint: *suncheo*] their language there." The multiplicity of nations represented at Pentecost is another link to Babel. Each nation had a national language. More importantly, all those nations referred to in Acts 2:9–11 had been disinherited by Yahweh when they were divided.
>
> The other word of importance (*diamerizo*; v. 3) is also used in the Septuagint, but not in Genesis 11. It is found exactly where one would expect it if one were

thinking in cosmic-geographical terms—Deuteronomy 32:8 (Septuagint: "When the Most High *divided* [*diamerizo*] the nations, when he scattered humankind, he fixed the boundaries of the nations"). This is a strong indication that Luke is drawing on the Septuagint, and specifically the Tower of Babel story in Genesis 11 and Deuteronomy 32:8–9, to describe the events on Pentecost.[24]

The inheritance of the nations involved the gathering of Gentiles together with the Jews that occurred all throughout the book of Acts. Notice these passages that say that the evangelism of Acts is the very fulfillment of the promise to gather the Gentiles with the Jews as his people:

Acts 15:13–19
After they finished speaking, James replied, "Brothers, listen to me. Simeon has related how God first visited the Gentiles, to take from them a people for his name. And with this the words of the prophets agree, just as it is written.

Acts 26:23
[Paul:] "that the Christ must suffer and that, by being the first to rise from the dead, he would proclaim light both to our people and to the Gentiles."

The "ingathering" of Gentiles with Jews was based upon unity of belief in Jesus as Messiah. Isaiah had prophesied that when Messiah first came (the branch of Jesse), *in that very day*, the Lord would "recover the remnant that remains of his people" from all the nations. "In that day," the root of Jesse would be "raised [resurrected] as a signal for the nations," and would "assemble the banished of Israel and gather the

---

[24] Michael S. Heiser, *The Unseen Realm: Recovering the Supernatural Worldview of the Bible*, First Edition (Bellingham, WA: Lexham Press, 2015), 298.

dispersed of Judah from the four corners of the earth" (Isa 11:1-2, 10-12). *In that day* of Messiah's arrival and resurrection (his raising as a signal), he would draw both the remnant of Israel as well as Gentile believers.

Paul likened that raising of the signal to Christ's resurrection and confirmed this Isaianic promise as already being fulfilled *during his ministry*:

> Romans 15:8–9, 12
> For I tell you that Christ became a servant to the circumcised to show God's truthfulness, in order to confirm the promises given to the patriarchs, and in order that the Gentiles might glorify God for his mercy…And again Isaiah says, "The root of Jesse will come, even he who arises to rule the Gentiles; in him will the Gentiles hope.

What were the promises given to the patriarchs that Paul says were confirmed ("verified") in Christ's resurrection? All of them, including the regathering (Acts 3:24; 32; 15:13-15; 24:24; 26:6). In fact, most of the prophecies about the regathering of Israel almost always add the inclusion of Gentiles as a simultaneous event.

Some Christians argue that God is currently bringing in the Gentiles, but he has yet to regather Israel. But Paul writes explicitly that the Isaianic prophecy about the gathering of the remnant *along with* the Gentiles was already being fulfilled *in his own day*, not in some distant future.

The Last Days of the Old Covenant

Back to Pentecost. In Acts 2, Peter then preaches a sermon about how this baptism of the Spirit meant that they were in the last days as Joel described, a time when the "Day of the Lord" was coming for Israel.

That Day of the Lord was the destruction of Jerusalem and the temple in AD 70. This has to be the case because Peter clearly states that the "last days" and "Day of the Lord" of Joel were being fulfilled in AD 30, not in a distant future (Acts 2:16). See my book *End Times Bible Prophecy* for the details on this.

> Acts 2:15–17
> For these people are not drunk, as you suppose, since it is only the third hour of the day. But <u>this is what was uttered through the prophet Joel:</u> " 'And in the <u>last days</u> it shall be, God declares, that I will pour out my Spirit on all flesh…

There could be no more explicit claim of Joel's "last days" being fulfilled in their day than Peter saying, "This is what was uttered through the prophet Joel." *This is* what was uttered. Not "this is yet to come," or "this *is like* what was uttered." ***This is*** what was uttered—or prophesied.

Pentecost was the beginning of the promise of God's outpoured Spirit, and it meant they were in the last days *in the first century.*

So the last days are not the last days of earth or of history. They must be the last days of something else.

The rest of Joel that Peter also quotes predicts the Day of the Lord. Christians tend to assume that the Day of the Lord is a reference to a universal end-of-time judgment. But in the Bible, it is not. In the Bible, "Day of the Lord" is used to describe a variety of local judgments by God on nations, peoples or cities (Zeph 1:7-15; Isa 13:6-19). So in their ancient Jewish mindset, every time a city, people or nation was judged by God, it was called "the Day of the Lord" for that local historical entity. Modern Christians tend to impose their own cultural bias, removed by thousands of years and thousands of miles, upon the text to make "Day of the Lord" mean the end of history judgment of all people that have ever existed. That's just not how the ancient mind thought.

The Day of the Lord to which Peter refers in Acts 2 is not a worldwide universal judgment but rather the localized national and city judgment of God. And what city or people were going to be judged in the coming Day of the Lord? Jesus said it would be Israel and her city and temple in Jerusalem (Matt 23:37-24:2; 21:37-45; 22:1-9; Luke 19:41-44).

Jesus described the Day of the Lord for Israel in his generation. He called it the "days of vengeance," with "wrath upon his people." That Day of the Lord was Yahweh using the Romans to destroy the holy city and temple in AD 70 because that generation of Jews as a whole did not accept the "time of the visitation" of Messiah (Luke 19:43-44). That was not a prophecy about some distant future, it was a prophecy that was fulfilled within a generation, within forty years—just like Jesus predicted (Matt 23:36; 24:34).

> Luke 21:20–24
> "But when you see Jerusalem surrounded by armies, then know that its desolation has come near. Then let those who are in Judea flee to the mountains, and let those who are inside the city depart, and let not those who are out in the country enter it, for these are days of vengeance, to fulfill all that is written. Alas for women who are pregnant and for those who are nursing infants in those days! For there will be great distress upon the earth and wrath against this people. They will fall by the edge of the sword and be led captive among all nations, and Jerusalem will be trampled underfoot by the Gentiles, until the times of the Gentiles are fulfilled.

Messiah would arrive in the last days of the old covenant to bring the new covenant, making the first obsolete. It was the age of Messiah that brought an end to the previous ages. And the historical event that marked the end of that old covenant age was the destruction of the old covenant temple and judgment of those who refused to let it go (I detail this historical fulfillment fully in narrative form in my novel series Chronicles of the Apocalypse).

The apostles said explicitly that they were in the last days, *in their own day*—also referred to as the "end of the ages":

> Hebrews 1:1–2
> Long ago, at many times and in many ways, God spoke to our fathers by the prophets, but in these last days he has spoken to us by his Son, whom he appointed the heir of all things.

> Hebrews 9:26
> for then [Jesus] would have had to suffer repeatedly since the foundation of the world. But as it is, he has appeared once for all at the end of the ages to put away sin by the sacrifice of himself.

> 1 Corinthians 10:11
> Now these things happened to them [in the old testament] as an example, but they were written down for our instruction, on whom the end of the ages has come.

The New Testament repeatedly states that those who lived in the first century were in the last days, or the end of the age(s). The Hebrews 9:26 verse says that Jesus' sacrifice on the cross marked the purpose of that age. His death and resurrection would herald the arrival of the Messianic age to come to which Jews everywhere looked forward. The last days or end of the age, were the last days of the old covenant because the Messiah brought in the new covenant age.

The common Jewish understanding was that there were basically two ages, the present age and the age to come, the age of Messiah. They were living in the "present age" that would be replaced by the messianic age to come (see 1 Tim 6:17; Titus 2:12; Heb 9:8-9; Eph 1:21; 1 Cor 2:6-8; Matt 12:32).

The old covenant age was the "present age" that would vanish when its symbol, the earthly Jerusalem temple, was destroyed. The writer of Hebrews knew this because Jesus said it would happen (Matt 24:1-2), and the author was writing before the temple was destroyed. So he likened the old covenant and its earthly temple to a temporary tabernacle that was about to vanish away.

> Hebrews 8:13
>
> In speaking of a new covenant, he makes the first one obsolete. And what is becoming obsolete and growing old is ready to vanish away.

He was writing during the transition period between covenants. The old covenant was becoming obsolete and was ready to vanish away, which means it had not yet done so. The new covenant had been inaugurated spiritually with the cross (Luke 22:20) but not yet consummated temporally in the destruction of the old covenant and its temple.

> Hebrews 9:8–9
>
> By this the Holy Spirit indicates that the way into the [heavenly] holy places is not yet opened as long as the first [earthly] tabernacle is still standing (which is symbolic for the present age).

Here, the writer of Hebrews explains that the earthly temple is symbolic of that present old covenant age that they were still in at the time of the writing of Hebrews, because that temple had not yet been destroyed. It was "still standing." When it was destroyed, it would mark the end of the present age and the full arrival of the Messianic age to come, the reign of Messiah on his heavenly throne.

Therefore, the last days could not have been the last days of the whole earth but rather the last days of the old covenant, the end of the old covenant age.[25]

And those last days/end of the age would include the destruction of the spiritual powers over the nations that were a part of that old covenant Deuteronomy 32 worldview. The passage I have referenced in previous chapters about the Watchers being "doomed to pass away" was also predicted by Paul to occur at the end of the age. They were in fact, the "rulers of this age" that was about to end with the temple destruction.

> 1 Corinthians 2:6
> …the rulers of this age, who are doomed to pass away.

As I explained earlier, 2 Peter 3 describes those last days as the Day of the Lord, when the *stoicheia* (the elemental spirits over the nations) would be burned up in judgment along with unbelieving sinners (Rev 20:15; 21:8).

The judgment of the Watchers that Jude said would occur at "the judgment of the great day" (Jude 6) occurred in AD 70 with the destruction of the old covenant and all its earthly and spiritual elements. *Space does not permit an explanation of how 2 Peter and Revelation were fulfilled in the first century (see my book End Times Bible Prophecy).*

Now the last days of Isaiah 2 makes more sense. Messiah arrived in the last days of the old covenant to usher in the mountain of the kingdom of God (Dan 2:44-45), accepting the Gentiles that were previously under the authority of the Watchers.

> Isaiah 2:2
> It shall come to pass in the last days [of the old covenant] that the mountain of the house of the LORD

---

[25] See "Chapter 9: End of the Age/Last Days," Brian Godawa, *End Times Bible Prophecy: It's Not What They Told You* (Embedded Pictures, 2017), 70-80.

shall be established as the highest of the mountains,
and shall be lifted up above the hills; <u>and all the nations
shall flow to it</u>...

That messianic mountain was also predicted by Daniel to begin in the
time of the Roman Empire with the coming of Messiah as a heavenly
cornerstone of a kingdom that would overcome all kingdoms and grow
to be a mountain that filled the earth (Dan 2:35, 44-45). Jesus was that
stone who came in the time of ancient Rome (Acts 4:11), his kingdom
was established in the first century (Matt 12:28), and it is currently
growing to fill the earth (Matt 13:31-33), just as Daniel prophesied.

All About the Narrative

So here is the summary narrative of what I have sought to exegete from
Psalm 82 in conjunction with the rest of Scripture:

• The Watchers had been allotted the Gentile nations in their ancient
rebellion and God kept Israel as his own allotment.

• But in the last days of the old covenant, Messiah came to take back
that inheritance.

• His death, resurrection and ascension to the right hand of God was his
enthronement that empowered him to overthrow the Watchers and
take back their territorial rights over the Gentile nations.

• He then regathered his remnant of Jews from all the nations through
the gospel proclamation of his new covenant kingdom.

• But this spiritual inauguration of the kingdom was not historically
consummated until the old covenant temple was destroyed.

• That new covenant now includes the Gentiles, no longer in bondage
to the powers, who now flow into the heavenly Mount Zion, the New
Jerusalem, the Body of Christ.

- There are no longer territorial Watchers who have power over the nations because Christ vanquished them through the cross, resurrection and ascension.

- At that time, he took back their inheritance and judged them by stripping them of immortality and most likely casting them into the lake of fire.

- He did this in the first century when the old covenant that included the Gentile allotment was completely abolished at the destruction of the old covenant temple in AD 70.

But we are still not done with this examination of Psalm 82. There is one other ramification to address in light of this narrative: If those spiritual principalities and powers were defeated and maybe even destroyed in the past, then how are we to understand the demonic evil that seems to plague our modern world?

That will be explored in the next chapter.

Chapter 6:
The Watchers Did Not Make You Do it

Having supported the supernatural interpretation of the gods of Psalm 82, I now want to address one of the tendencies that I see occurring within the community of those persuaded by the divine council worldview. They are often so focused on the heavenly principalities and powers that they can fall into a misunderstanding of human responsibility for evil in this world.

Since the Sons of God are understood within this view as being supernatural beings, then the interpretation of Genesis 6:1-4 places some of the cause of the great Flood upon the actions of those angelic divinities.

In that controversial passage, rebellious supernatural Sons of God come to earth and mate with human women in a violation of the heavenly/earthly divide (Jude 6-7). Their progeny were the cursed Nephilim, to whom the Bible links the cursed giants of Canaan (Num 13:32-33) (I can't take the space here to prove that interpretation. See my book *When Giants Were Upon the Earth* for the biblical evidence).

But the context of that Genesis 6 passage is that the physical corruption by the heavenly beings was part of the reason for the judgment of the flood.

> Genesis 6:11–13
> Now the land was <u>corrupt</u> in God's sight, and the land was filled with violence. And God saw the land, and behold, it was <u>corrupt</u>, for <u>all flesh had corrupted</u> their way on the land. And God said to Noah, "I have determined to make an end of <u>all flesh</u>, for the land is

filled with violence through them. Behold, I will destroy them with the land.

Though the Bible gives no details beyond the violence and "corruption" of flesh, some Bible researchers draw from 1 Enoch to fill in the gaps of knowledge left out in Genesis. I've already explained that though 1 Enoch is not Scripture, it is certainly a source used by Scripture, so it carries some weight when it comes to understanding biblical context.

In 1 Enoch, we read an extended exposition of Genesis 6. It tells us that the Sons of God, also called the Watchers, were guilty of teaching mankind the arts of wickedness, from adultery and war, to sorcery, astrology and other forbidden dark arts.

> 1 Enoch 7:1-8:4
> And [the Watchers] took wives unto themselves, and everyone (respectively) chose one woman for himself, and they began to go unto them. And they taught them magical medicine, incantations, the cutting of roots...And Azaz'el taught the people (the art of) making swords and knives, and shields, and breastplates; ...and alchemy. And there were many wicked ones and they committed adultery and erred, and all their conduct became corrupt... And (the people) cried and their voice reached unto heaven.[26]

1 Enoch paints a picture of humanity maliciously influenced by Watchers before the Flood. That means that the Watchers had some responsibility for the corruption that filled the land with violence (Gen 6:11). Under the Deuteronomy 32 worldview, the Old Testament extends that evil influence after Babel and all the way up to the arrival of Messiah.

---

[26] James H. Charlesworth, *The Old Testament Pseudepigrapha, vol. 1* (New York; London: Yale University Press, 1983), 16.

But if what I am saying is true, that the Watchers are not only disinherited from the nations, but have been judged and possibly even destroyed in the first century AD, then that would mean that they are no longer active in this world.

Supernatural Evil or Human Evil?

One of the most common questions I get from those who are following my argument is that if what I say is true, then how do I explain the great evil that this world still experiences, from world wars to genocides? Certainly, that is demonic, is it not? And how do I explain all the apparent demonic activity that still seems to captivate our world? Even if we dismiss the charlatan exorcists and psychological explanations of many alleged supernatural cases, there still seems to be real apparent demonic activity in our world. How can that be if there are no demonic gods over the nations? And besides, didn't Paul write about the very real struggle going on with "principalities and powers" after the resurrection and ascension of Christ? (Eph 6;12). Isn't Satan spoken of as still being the Prince of the power of the air (Eph 2:2), the "god of this world" (2 Cor 4:4)?

My first charge is that despite the real evil that the Watchers did in the cosmos, they are still not the cause of evil inside human hearts. We are. A Watcher didn't make Cain commit the first homicide that typified our murderous human nature.

The Watchers may have been part of the reason for the Flood, they may have *influenced* humanity, but they were not *the cause* of human evil. That was found in humanity's own depravity.

> Genesis 6:5–6
> The LORD saw that the wickedness of man was great in the land, and that every intention of the thoughts of his heart was only evil continually. And the LORD regretted

that he had made man on the land, and it grieved him to
his heart.

The text indicates that the wickedness and evil of humanity resided in
their own hearts, not outside of them in other beings. We are not puppets
of someone else's evil.

But there is something else to notice in Genesis 6. Though the behavior of
the Sons of God is implicated, it is not explicitly stated as the reason for
the flood. The text goes out of its way to focus emphatically on the
"wickedness and evil heart of man" as God's main motive for the flood,
without any reference to the Sons of God/Watchers. God makes "an end
of all flesh, for the land is filled with violence through them" (Gen 6:11).
The focus in Genesis is on the evil caused by humans (flesh) not Watchers.

Even in the most wicked period of history, God does not shift the blame
of monstrous world evil onto external demonic spiritual forces. The
heavenly and earthly are linked in both behavior and fates, but God
blames the evil inside the human heart on humanity.

The wicked heart of man is a common refrain throughout the Old Testament,
highlighting an internal origin of human evil, not an external one.

> Genesis 8:21
> The intention of man's heart is evil from his youth...

> Jeremiah 17:9
> The heart is deceitful above all things, and desperately
> sick; who can understand it?
> (see also Job 14:4; 15:14; Ps. 51:5; Jer 13:23)

The New Testament picks up this notion of internal sin nature and
reaffirms it even after the kingdom of God has come in the new
covenant.

James 1:13–15
Let no one say when he is tempted, "I am being
tempted by God," for God cannot be tempted with evil,
and he himself tempts no one. But each person is
tempted <u>when he is lured and enticed by his own
desire</u>. <u>Then desire when it has conceived gives birth to
sin, and sin when it is fully grown brings forth death.</u>

External forces can tempt us, but in the chain of causation, we are the
originating source of our evil. Human nature does not need Watchers to
explain the heinous "demonic" evil of world wars, genocide and other
atrocities that saturate our newspapers and history books. We can
accomplish all of that on our own.

Adolf Hitler, Josef Stalin, Mao, Dahmer, Bundy, Gacy, the 9/11
terrorists and their successors; none of them needed to be demon-
possessed to do what they did. As Jesus said, "For out of [man's] heart
come evil thoughts, murder, adultery, sexual immorality, theft, false
witness, slander."

Paul wrote a long list of human depravity that comes from the human
"lust of our own hearts" and "debased minds." No demons or Watchers
required.

Romans 1:29–32
[Sinful humanity is] filled with all manner of
unrighteousness, evil, covetousness, malice. They are
full of envy, murder, strife, deceit, maliciousness. They
are gossips, slanderers, haters of God, insolent,
haughty, boastful, inventors of evil, disobedient to
parents, foolish, faithless, heartless, ruthless. Though
they know God's righteous decree that those who
practice such things deserve to die, they not only do
them but give approval to those who practice them.

Again, this is an internal wickedness so thorough that no external supernatural entity is needed to explain it. It comes from within the heart of unredeemed humanity. And Paul was no stranger to demonic reality. He knew demons when he saw them (Acts 16:16-18; 19:12; Eph 6:12). But he didn't explain the worst of human wickedness by appealing to them in Romans 1.

If one thinks that the disinheriting of the Watchers' authority over nations means that there is no explanation for the evil in humanity, then perhaps one has forgotten that human evil is not located in heavenly beings but in humans themselves.

What the Devil is Going On Here?

This doesn't mean there are no demons or evil spirits anymore. Watchers are not demons; they are a separate category of beings from demons. Demons are evil spirits in search of a human host (Luke 11:24-25). But Watchers are not merely spirits, they are angelic divine rulers with heavenly flesh (Jude 7-8) that can fornicate with humans (Gen 6:1-4) and eat food (Gen 18:8). Watchers are *not* pure spirit like demons.

Watchers are more like generals in a spiritual war, and demons are like the troops. Assassinating the generals doesn't necessarily destroy the troops.

Just because the Watchers have been conquered or destroyed does not mean that there are no more evil spirits. I am not aware of any biblical description of evil spirits being destroyed from the earth, so I am agnostic on the issue. But I know that if there are demons, they are not Watchers or "rulers, authorities and cosmic powers in the heavenly places" that Paul wrote about in his day (Eph 6:12). Those were the Watchers of the nations.

Jesus said that the eternal fire was made for the devil and his angels (Matt 25:41), and since "angels" in Greek means messengers, it most likely includes demons. But Jesus' parables about Gehenna seem to only mention humans being thrown there at the end of the age (AD 70). I am not aware of any passage that directly says when the demons will end up there, so we would have to speculate as to when. They may still be around today. But that would make them more like terrorist cells without any central command.

It seems reasonable that the demons would be thrown into the Lake of Fire along with Satan at the end of the Millennium. But it is not explicitly written so (Rev 20:10).

Don't Forget

But what about Paul's reference to spiritual powers in his epistles such as Ephesians 6? Isn't the satan still the god of this world like the New Testament says? As we already discussed, those letters were written in the "last days" of the old covenant (Heb 1:1-2), before the temple had been destroyed and before the new covenant kingdom had been historically consummated. So the Watchers had been legally disinherited, paraded in Triumph, but not yet judged or executed. That would come with the final earthly destruction of the old covenant.

Remember, the temple was the incarnation of the old covenant. Its earthly presence marked the presence of that covenant still on earth. And the old covenant included the territorial spiritual powers as part of its paradigm (Deut 32:8-10). So if the old covenant was still in effect on earth until that temple destruction in AD 70 (Heb 9:8-9), then the Watchers were still at war with Yahweh and his Messiah during the transition period between covenants (Heb 8:13).

But when Jesus abolished the old covenant by destroying the earthly temple, he received the new covenant kingdom and the Watchers lost their power and were judged with the fire of execution They were burned up as *stoicheia*.

And that brings us to the next issue.

The Already and the Not Yet

Another attempt at addressing the apparent presence of supernatural evil in our modern world in the face of Christ's defeat and disinheritance of the Watchers is the suggestion that Christ's victory and triumphal procession was a legal or spiritual reality that is now being worked out historically.

What that means is that there can still be evil supernatural entities who have power over sinful humanity, but have limited power in relation to the Gospel. So, they may not have authority, but they still have power. Much like a criminal has no legal authority, but may have power in doing evil. This is commonly coined "the already and the not yet" explanation.

I actually believe there is some truth to this theological concept. But I don't think it provides a satisfactory answer to the question of the Watchers. Let me explain.

Here is the basic argument: Jesus Christ has indeed triumphed over the spiritual powers and has been enthroned as king over all the nations. Everything is under his feet, but this is only a legal or theological truth that is still working its way out in history.

Therefore, even though Christ has been victorious, the spiritual powers still rule over the nations, but Christ is exercising his superior rule over their rule by saving Gentiles from the nations. He is reigning *now* from heaven, but this is a spiritual sovereignty that is *not yet* historically incarnate on earth. It will be so in our future. It is gradually replacing the "already" with the "not yet"–step by step.

One Scripture that seems to teach this "already and not yet" is Hebrews 2.

Hebrews 2:7–8
You made [Jesus] for a little while lower than the
angels; you have crowned him with glory and honor,
putting everything in subjection under his feet." Now in
putting everything in subjection to him, he left nothing
outside his control. At present, we do not yet see
everything in subjection to him.

The writer of Hebrews affirms the prophetic fulfillment of the messianic enthronement Psalm 110 (everything under his feet), but explicitly qualifies that as a heavenly truth that is in process historically ("at present, we do not yet see everything in subjection to him"). It is spiritually true but historically coming true. The already (heavenly) and the not yet (earthly).

Here is another passage that expounds on this historical "process" of subjugation:

1 Corinthians 15:24–27
Then comes the end, when [Jesus] delivers the
kingdom to God the Father after destroying every rule
and every authority and power. For he must reign until
he has put all his enemies under his feet. The last
enemy to be destroyed is death. For "God has put all
things in subjection under his feet."

I cannot exegete the entire complex chapter of 1 Corinthians 15, so I will just explain that I understand this to be referring to the end of history, when Christ returns. The idea here is that Christ is reigning right now from his heavenly throne at the right hand of God with all things legally or covenantally under his feet (Eph 1:20-22).

Jesus then makes true on earth what is already true in heaven (Matt 18:19), step by step, subject by subject. He has already conquered the spiritual authorities and executed them, but now, he is conquering the humans that used to be under their authority through Gospel conversion.

This is much like an earthly king who reigns over a nation whether the people like it or not. As he employs his power, he gets his subjects to obey him, until they are all willing in their loyalty to the king.

But remember, the kingdom of God is not of this world (John 18:36); it is a spiritual kingdom (Luke 17:21). Its "conquering" is a spiritual conquering through conversion, not earthly compulsion. As people receive the Holy Spirit and are brought into God's kingdom, they become his subjects "under his feet" historically.

Jesus enacts his reign by working out in history what is already true in the heavenlies. As more people convert and are placed under his feet, the kingdom of God grows to be a mountain that fills the whole earth (Dan 2:35). It begins as a small speck of leaven, but soon expands to leaven the whole lump of dough (Luke 13:20). It starts as the smallest seed but grows to be the largest tree in the garden (Luke 13:19). So, while the kingdom is spiritual in its operations, it is earthly in its ramifications.

So, doesn't this support the notion that the Watchers may still have power without authority?

No. And here's why…

As we have already seen, the actual New Testament texts use the Roman Triumph as the picture of what occurred through the ascension of Christ and his judgment of AD 70. That picture was one of execution of the prisoners not release of them back into the nations. The forty-year transition period with old and new covenants overlapping explains how the principalities and powers were still around at that time. Because even though the new covenant had been inaugurated in the heavenly realm, the earthly old covenant temple still stood, so the old covenant still had some earthly effect. But with the destruction of the temple, so came the final destruction of the old covenant along with the Watchers. Their authority *and* power was rooted in the old covenant.

1 Corinthians 15:24-27 describes the *historical process* of Jesus "destroying every rule and authority and power." But it is a process that involves not merely the already and the not yet, but also the "before now." In other words, it involves the past, the present and the future.

The historical order is this:

1) Jesus disinherited the spiritual powers at his ascension and placed all authorities under his feet in the heavenly realm. The earthly fulfillment of that heavenly accomplishment is the destruction of the old covenant and temple in AD 70. That heavenly "already" eventually overcame and replaced the earthly "not yet" with the historical judgment of AD 70, and that heavenly "already" will continue to do so until God's will is fully done on earth as it is in heaven (Matt 6:10).

2) Jesus is now in the historical process of placing all humans under his feet on earth through spiritual conversion. On earth as it is in heaven.

3) Jesus will destroy the last enemy, death, at the end of history.

Past, present, future.

So, yes, there is an "already and not yet" aspect of heavenly truth and earthly impact, but the "not yet" does not include the Watchers because, as we have already seen in previous chapters, the spiritual powers were already conquered *in the heavenly realm*, where they resided. The heavenly realm is the "already." The earthly realm of history was the "not yet" that was fulfilled in the temple destruction. Final execution of the spiritual powers is part of the past accomplishment of Jesus' Days of Vengeance (Luke 21:20-22) in AD 70. The Watchers were triumphantly dragged through the streets, shamed, and disinherited from their allotments (Col 2:15). Then they were judged by being cast into the Lake of Fire in AD 70 with the destruction of the old covenant. As Psalm 82:7 says, they lost their immortality and died like any other prince. They're gone.

The rule of the Watchers is part of the old covenant that Messiah did away with. The heavenly realm is accomplished; it is the remaining "not yet" aspects of the earthly realm that continue to occur historically.

The Watchers were already conquered and destroyed. Their corresponding earthly powers are currently being conquered. Death will ultimately be conquered.

Amen.

• • • • •

To see how the rule of the fallen Watchers over the Gentile nations may have played out in history, read my novel series, *Chronicles of the Nephilim* and *Chronicles of the Watchers*.

To see what the Watcher's final destruction might have looked like, read my series *Chronicles of the Apocalypse*.

For more theological explanation of the last days and eschatology see my book *End Times Bible Prophecy.*

If you liked this book, then please help me out by writing an honest review of it on Amazon here. It's usually pretty easy. That is one of the best ways to say thank you to me as an author. It really does help my exposure and status as an author. Thanks! — *Brian Godawa*

• • • • •

Great Offers by Brian Godawa

Get More Biblical Imagination

Sign up Online For

The Godawa Chronicles

Https://godawa.com

Updates and Freebies of the Books of Brian Godawa

Special Discounts, Free Articles,
Cool Artwork and Videos!

About the Author

Brian Godawa is the screenwriter for the award-winning feature film, *To End All Wars,* starring Kiefer Sutherland. It was awarded the Commander in Chief Medal of Service, Honor and Pride by the Veterans of Foreign Wars, won the first Heartland Film Festival by storm, and showcased the Cannes Film Festival Cinema for Peace.

He also co-wrote *Alleged,* starring Brian Dennehy as Clarence Darrow and Fred Thompson as William Jennings Bryan. He previously adapted to film the best-selling supernatural thriller novel *The Visitation* by author Frank Peretti for Ralph Winter (*X-Men, Wolverine*), and wrote and directed *Wall of Separation,* a PBS documentary, and *Lines That Divide*, a documentary on stem cell research.

Mr. Godawa's scripts have won multiple awards in respected screenplay competitions, and his articles on movies and philosophy have been published around the world. He has traveled around the United States teaching on movies, worldviews, and culture to colleges, churches and community groups.

His popular book, *Hollywood Worldviews: Watching Films with Wisdom and Discernment* (InterVarsity Press) is used as a textbook in schools around the country. His novel series, the saga *Chronicles of the Nephilim* is in the Top 10 of Biblical Fiction on Amazon and is an imaginative retelling of Biblical stories of the Nephilim giants, the secret plan of the fallen Watchers, and the War of the Seed of the Serpent with the Seed of Eve. The sequel series, *Chronicles of the Apocalypse* tells the story of the Apostle John's book of Revelation, and *Chronicles of the Watchers* recounts true history through the Watcher paradigm.

Find out more about his other books, lecture tapes and dvds for sale at his website https://godawa.com/.

Made in the USA
Middletown, DE
17 February 2023

25068598R00060